The heart of work

Celebrating
30 Years of Publishing
in India

Praise for *The Heart of Work*

Stories are considered as tools for communication between two minds, and this book shares inspirational real-life stories that are easy to read and comprehend. The magical quality is that it will transform your life and your relationship with people around you.

After reading just a few stories, I knew that this book is a companion of mine for a lifetime.

— Sandeep Bakshi, MD and CEO, ICICI Bank

This book can be called a masterpiece owing to the human library that it includes, with each human/one of us being a book full of life-stories and experiences. It goes beyond the heart of work and delves deep in the subconscious and at the level of the soul, leading to a certain degree of self-reflection and contemplation. The impressions formed through childhood and career have been expressed in a very simple heart-touching manner, breaking down the complexities of intellect, education and success.

— Deepak Mangla, CEO, Corporate Centers, India and Philippines and member, Asia-Pacific Management Committee, J.P. Morgan

Nathan keeps alive the story-telling tradition of India in context of the organized corporate sector. He weaves participant observation and personalization in a unique way to deliver insights and lessons that take a professional a lifetime to experience and gather. This, indeed, is a new genre of management writing that is valuable for anyone who wants a different take on the substance of effective membership and leadership in organizations.

— Santrupt Misra, Group Director, Birla Carbon; Director, Chemicals; Director, Group HR, Aditya Birla Group

Nathan's *The Heart of Work* is like a beautiful garland with fragrant flowers from the garden of life, bound together with the string of mindfulness. It comprises vignettes of distilled wisdom, imparting lessons through stories that are simple in expression and profound in impact. It brings alive veritable moments from Nathan's own career and life that have shaped him.

Stories, told well, are a part of the human condition and have the power to change lives. This book is an invaluable read for both, aspiring and seasoned professionals in the corporate world, on how one can be an effective manager and a good leader. It also serves as an engaging primer for parents and educators to impart vital life lessons to students.

— N.S. Rajan, former Group CHRO and member, Group Executive Council, Tata Sons

This book is unique, as each story is distinct and different. They are deep and meaningful, and the best part is that one can see themselves in these stories. The messages conveyed are powerful and relevant even for a lay person. They are also a reflection of the humane, empathetic and insightful personality of the author. I enjoyed reading them and I wish the reader would enjoy them as much as I did.

— P.R. Ramesh, former Chairman, Deloitte India

Nathan's opus *The Heart of Work* is a delightful collection of heart-warming stories, narrated in a light, breezy style. In a world fatigued by preachy and heavy management articles, replete with mind-numbing jargon, Nathan's book truly comes as a breath of fresh air. It has great potency to make readers think and imbibe his life lessons as if they are their own.

— S. Venkatesh, member, Group Management Board and President, Group HR, RPG Enterprises

Nathan's stories are largely filled with a human touch. He narrates incidents in an interesting way; they are absorbing and difficult to leave once you start. I am glad Nathan is publishing his experiences and imagination in the form of this book. I am confident that it will be a great contribution to all generations of people and managers and, particularly, those in the people management or HR field.

—T.V. Rao, former professor, IIMA; L&T Professor, XLRI

I've always believed that life is the best school and our experiences, the best teacher. Some experiences leave an everlasting impression on us, some make us wiser, some have the power to change our perspective and outlook towards life or situations and some others inspire us to be a better version of ourselves, both personally and professionally. This book by my dear friend, Nathan, is a potpourri of experiences that have shaped his approach in life and as a leader. As I read through these stories, what got me hooked was not just the simplicity with which they have been told, but the compelling life lesson each one offers.

— Lakshmi Chandrasekharan, India HR Lead, Accenture

If you have interacted with Nathan, you will know what an entertaining storyteller he is. And when the stories are based on varied incidents from his life and profession, I am sure it will make for an interesting read. Glad that he chose to share his life lessons with a wider audience.

— Gangapriya Chakraverti, India Site Head and MD, Ford India

It is not often that the work of a debutant author rivets the reader to his book and brings an occasional smile. SV Nathan's *The Heart of Work* is one such book.

It is a treasure trove of anecdotes carefully chosen from Nathan's well-lived life. Small yet significant events have been beautifully narrated in the pen picture that the author draws with ease. Brevity has been leveraged powerfully to hold the readers' attention, and complete disregard for connecting one story with the next adds authenticity and spontaneity. Stories are endearing and, at the same time, demonstrate the author's deep understanding of the human mind as well as heart. Each story touches that chord in the reader that evokes empathy, respect and even humour.

This book certainly will not need a bookmark because it will be challenging to put it down midway through reading various stories.

—Aquil Busrai, CEO, Aquil Busrai Consulting; former Executive Director, HR, Shell Malaysia and IBM India

We often wonder how some of the iconic leaders of our times evolved their signature leadership style and inspirational impact. We try and guess some of these by watching leaders in action or discussing situations with them to draw upon their perspectives and insight. More often than not, a leader's style is a result of the shaping experiences they have had in life's journey, which left an imprint on their heart and shaped how they showed up in life and at work!

However, it is rare for leaders to make the time to curate those stories and hand it over to the next generation in a distilled fashion.

The Heart of Work is one such distilled essence—a compendium of experiences that shaped the leader that we see as Nathan today.

— Mahalakshmi R., Head HR, South East Asia, Mondelēz International

Only people with empathy and a keen sense of observation can find meaning and wisdom in everyday situations. In *The Heart of Work*, master storyteller SV Nathan draws from his rich experience to tell many such stories with great sensitivity and a touch of humour. A great way for professionals to learn soft skills—so essential in the workplace.

— Anita Bhogle, partner, Prosearch Consultants; author, *The Winning Way*

Nathan's book serves us a slice-of-life compilation of his personal discoveries and experiences that have shaped his professional career, values and worldview. His keen observation, sensitivity and openness are imprinted in these anecdotes. His master story-telling skills are evident in the effortless flow of the stories and the quiet reflection it compels you to indulge in. All of us have had these pivotal moments where there are lessons to be gained, if one is willing to look for them. This book truly emphasizes and places the human experience at the heart of work.

— Hema Ravichandar, strategic HR advisor

This unique book provides a graphic account of authentic life lessons that the author himself learnt along the way as he traversed through a successful career over the years. These inspiring stories are a must-read for any professional committed to building an exciting future ahead in a meaningful way.

— Arvind Agarwal, managing partner, Lead Associates

This is an extremely precious book, more so because it's coming from Nathan, who is one of the most celebrated leaders in HR. I am sure this book will be an extremely useful guide for every professional—not only in HR but also beyond! A book with many practical insights, inspiration and tips making it even more helpful.

— Prem Singh, President, Group HR, JK Group

Nathan has masterfully captured the emotion and the humanity behind these stories. These are stories from everyday life, over four decades, that any of us may have experienced. However, Nathan's attention to detail and vivid description bring these stories to life for each of us, along with great learning about people, relationships and humanity. These stories show us the magic of people and makes us reflect on how we might change our perspectives and behaviours to tap into this sea of human potential and power.

— **Krish Shankar, Group HR Head, Infosys**

Life is a beautiful journey to be experienced and not a problem to be dealt with. Live in the present and experience it in a way that positively changes the next day. This is what I learnt from Nathan as he shared his candid experiences in this book. He has described every experience so simply and beautifully that sums up how the destination of life is in the journey itself. A must-read for anyone at any age.

— **Anuranjita Kumar, founder and CEO, We-Ace**

Workplace is a theatre where we are playing out our inner story for more than half our waking hours. At work, all of us are shaping the world that we live in, but what if we were to turn our attention to a more pivotal question—how did this world of work, environment, culture and people shape us?

It is, indeed, humbling to introduce SV Nathan's personal collection of stories, *The Heart of Work*. Deeply personal, this book presents nuggets of learning, moments that mattered through a wonderful compilation of stories, seeking to answer the question of people and the culture shaping them. Stories remind us of our concerns about identity and relationships, our desires and our sense of self and our heritage. This book reminds us of our humanness, our similarities and the people who inspire and shape us every day.

And when you read a book by this master-craftsman, pour out your own cup, hold it out empty and fill it with stories.

— **Rajkamal Vempati, President and Head, Human Resources, Axis Bank**

Knowing Nathan for many years, as expected, he has poured his heart into this work. It is amazing that these short stories transport you into a setting where you see yourself in them … more power to him.

— Deepak Hota, former Chairman and Managing Director, BEML

Nathan has been a mentor to many and has shared many a story. He has an art of conveying his message with impact. This book is special as it has many stories from his journey. Inspiring and thought-provoking.

— Harjeet Khanduja, Senior Vice President, HR, Reliance Jio

The heart of work

HOW TO UNLOCK YOUR TRUE POTENTIAL USING THE POWER OF INSIGHT

SV NATHAN

HARPER BUSINESS

An Imprint of HarperCollins *Publishers*

First published in India by Harper Business
An imprint of HarperCollins *Publishers* 2022
4th Floor, Tower A, Building No 10, DLF Cyber City,
DLF Phase II, Gurugram, Haryana – 122002
www.harpercollins.co.in

2 4 6 8 10 9 7 5 3

P-ISBN: 978-93-5629-429-5
E-ISBN: 978-93-5629-430-1

Typeset in 11.5/14.5 Linden Hill
Manipal Technologies Limited, Manipal

Printed and bound at
Thomson Press (India) Ltd

MIX
Paper
FSC FSC® C010615

This book is produced from independently certified FSC® paper to ensure responsible forest management.

To the three women in my life—my grandmother,
my mother and my dear wife, Chitra

Contents

CAREER-BUILDING

CULTURE-BUILDING

HABITS AND BEHAVIOURS

LEADERSHIP

GETTING BETTER

Preface

On 6 June 2021, a friend called me up and asked me if my book was ready. I was caught off guard. What book? I was not sure if I had given any commitment to anyone about writing a book. I had always been thinking about writing a book, though—but just felt lazy about it. So, I had settled for writing a few blogs from time to time, the occasional story. What I enjoyed about them was how simple yet profound happenings shaped my outlook towards work and life.

Work, in more than one way, is an art. At the core, one's work is influenced not so much by the mind but by what beats between the third and the seventh ribs on the left—the heart.

We are shaped by what happens around us. I am told that the only organ that comes full-grown from the time a baby is born is the eyes. The eyes observe what happens around us and help experience the world in a certain way. The brain processes these stimuli and calls us to action. Somehow, in all this science, I feel that the heart is missed out. And yet, in all that we do, at times we listen to the mind and at times to the heart.

Work, overall, is about getting things done, and the heart does not normally figure in it. But in my many years of work, I have seen that the heart has a huge influence on what happens to us, what happens around us and what propels us to action.

So, I called up my friend and told him that I would have the book ready by the end of the year. I stuck to the plan. I compiled the many happenings of my life and career which had made an impact on me, and bundled them into a small set of readable pieces. Many incidents that had seemed so ordinary when they happened had afterwards blossomed into a world of profound wisdom for me. They were an anchor for me, and I found solace in them. I shared these stories at any opportunity I could find—in conversation with my friends, at colleges, in training programmes and at any forum where I spoke. I realized that my sharing them seemed to leave an impact on the audience. Stories are a powerful way of conveying an idea, which remains long after it is heard or read.

Over time, and upon constant nudging, I began to collect such incidents that were 'moments that mattered'. I was egged on to write a book. I stalled. The noise increased to such a pitch that, as I said, I made a commitment to write a book. I thank my many friends on social media who gently pushed me forward. I decided to complete the book by a certain date. I kept up that promise.

These moments that matter don't have a timeline. There is no date to a story. Just words that bind a happening. My grandma used to start her stories with 'once upon a time'. Her stories were magic. Their magic lay partly in the ending, as much as the cadence of it all. I could identify myself in them. That is the magic I felt with my stories. Not preachy, not pedantic, and yet touching the core of my being. They are about working from the heart. The heart of work. People learn through listening, reading and reflecting on the stories that convey messages in a subtle way. These moments that I have culled provided me a perspective. A moment that changed a perspective or brought a change within me and, in a few cases, within those around me. Much of this helped me shape my life and career. At the core of these stories are the values that bind them, the arteries and veins and tissues that bind the heart of work.

Work and career, by their very nature, are about building. Slowly, brick on mortar and upon a well-laid foundation. We are shaped by the experiences, and many of them stand out for the way they provide a strong anchor. The book is a compilation of stories of a journeyman's life into many significant events that provided insights that helped shape his life and career. Given that they have happened over a period of time, the instances are timeless in some ways. Some names have been changed to protect the identities of my co-passengers, and some have been retained. I am positive that they would recognize themselves in them. Most things that go through our minds, we forget, but those that touch the heart, we seldom forget. In all the work that I did, these did touch the core of my heart. They are fun to read and relatable, I am sure, for it is about any journeyman's life.

This book aims to help readers seek out their own stories that help them discover their own anchors of work. It is meant for a wide audience, for in a way, the journeyman has been through several roads to reach his destination. It is about the heart of work. I felt that these stories could be equally useful to a young professional, a mid-career professional and a senior professional. It addresses anyone who is curious about work and what drives them.

I hope it appeals to students, business professionals and anyone who is fond of light reading. The book will also appeal to teachers in business schools and to training professionals. It is a book where one can flick to a page, any page, and start reading any story, and it would still have meaning. It is easy on the reader. It is directed towards millennials and zennials, for they are always keen on feedback.

As you read this book, I invite you to stay with your personal experiences. Some of these musings will resonate with you for sure. Ask yourself why they hold an appeal in you. In that lies the meaning of your anchors, your motivation and your prime driver. I am positive you will start to collect stories in your life and discover the core of your work and your character. The heart of work. Happy reading.

Values at Work

Your beliefs become your thoughts,
Your thoughts become your words,
Your words become your actions,
Your actions become your habits,
Your habits become your values,
Your values become your destiny.

—M.K. Gandhi

Values are central to life and career-building. Whether it is about an opportunity given to another or a sense of fairness, or whether it is about giving a second chance to someone. Or doing something despite it being out of the way because it is the right thing to do. Much of life is about integrity and how we hold ourselves to the highest standards of ethics and eschew even the smallest distraction that could lead us astray. Values define us. We develop them by observing what others do, not what they say.

Values are not born with us. We imbue values from those around us—friends, peers, parents—and, given that we spend a lot of time at the workplace, from our co-workers. We sometimes surprise ourselves in the values that we hold unto ourselves—things that others tell us that they have experienced in us, or what we have experienced in them. Ultimately, when the penny drops, it is about what people remember the most, and often times, it is not from the part of the brain that holds our memories, but the part of the brain that holds our feelings. Yes, indeed.

1

Of Androcles and What Goes Around Comes Around

My grandmother taught me to read and write and instilled in me values, as all mothers and grandmas do. Of all the things I remember about my grandma, what I remember the most are her stories. She was just simply so absorbing in the words she crafted into each incident that we would get lost in them, transported to another world and living in that moment. That was special about her. I remember her telling me the story of Androcles and the lion. She described the forest, the cave and Androcles, the young man, a slave. Androcles was tortured by his cruel master, and he escaped from the clutches of his oppressor and ran away into the forest. He came near a cave, where he heard the roar of a lion that sounded different—more like a lion moaning and in pain.

He goes up to the cave and finds a lion roaring in pain and recognizes it needs help. Very gingerly, he moves towards it and sees that there is a thorn that is deeply embedded in the lion's paw. He musters his courage, goes up to the lion and speaks soothingly to it, and then removes the thorn. He tears a portion of cloth from his garment and uses it to bandage the wounded paw with some special healing leaves, and then goes his way.

Much later, Androcles gets caught and is thrown into the arena where runaway slaves are killed in a gruesome manner by setting lions on them. When the gates are opened, a lion that has not been fed for many days rushes towards him. However, instead of killing him, the lion licks his hands. It was the lion that Androcles had saved.

My grandmother used to recount the story with a lot of enthusiasm and spent a lot more time explaining the moral of the story—help people who are in trouble, and don't expect anything in return. If you do get a reward, it is a bonus, she would say. We used to ask her a lot of questions and she would patiently respond to each of them to say that it was most important to do the right thing. It always fascinated me, this ask of hers—do good, regardless. And to anyone who needed help. Do what is right.

Fast forward in time to about 1997. I was recruiting at a campus in Calcutta (now Kolkata) and made job offers to a few students. It is always a difficult task, this campus recruitment—a lot of effort: part selling the job and part selecting the best. About a couple of months later, one of the candidates whom we selected, I shall call him Sai—an outstanding candidate—called me to say that he could not join my organization. He said that he had failed to meet some requirement and that he would therefore not be getting his 'certification'. He was choking with tears. His mother gently took the phone and requested me to extend the validity of his appointment letter by six months, which would allow him to meet the college requirements. She was apologetic and asked for another chance for her son. She was obviously distraught.

I was in a bit of a quandary. One could bring a candidate only if they met the criteria. Although this was against policy, I took a view that we would allow for an extension that could have Sai join us in case he cleared his exams. His mother was happy, as was Sai. Six months later, Sai called me to say that he was very thankful that we had kept his offer valid for six months but could not join us, as he had found a job closer home. He said that the new job would keep his mother happy, as she would not have to travel to another city. He also said that the offer that was kept valid for him had given a big leg-up to his sagging confidence. I was very unhappy that he could not join us, but I could understand his predicament. All was forgiven and forgotten.

Fast forward to the year 2011. A colleague of mine called on me with a request to help him find a job for his wife, Sudha, a qualified salesperson working in a bank. I wrote to a good friend—let me call him Ram—a director in one of the largest Indian banking institutions, and asked him to consider her candidature on merit. Ram replied that he would try and forwarded my mail to his colleague, who would let me know of the outcome of the interviews.

A couple of months later, Sudha called me to say that she had got the job. The details got jumbled in her rush of words of excitement and gratitude, and I was thrilled that she got the job—it was all that mattered. I was very impressed that her resumé got the right attention at the right level and the speed at which it was evaluated, and an appointment letter issued, and in one of the prestigious banks!

I was still in wonderment of the speed of action on a resumé, when I got a call at my desk. It was from the bank, and a senior human resources (HR) professional wanted to speak to me. He mentioned that Sudha's resume came to him, and he had noted where the mail came from and had gone the extra mile to ensure that the resumé got the right attention. I thanked him profusely and observed that it was done at great speed. It was then that he said that I had not changed at all. I was now curious. I told him that I did not understand what he meant. He asked me if I remembered giving a helping hand to a candidate who had not met the university requirements and had kept the appointment letter valid as a special case. The penny dropped. Yes, how could I forget! It was Sai. I could not believe that I was speaking to Sai. Virtual hugs followed.

I put the phone down, humming Justin Timberlake's song 'What Goes Around Comes Around'. And I remembered my grandmother and the story of gratitude.

2

Of Math Tests and Second Chances

A profound insight into character building happened during my days in college. I used to be at Vivekananda College, Chennai—a revered institution. Those who graduated from Vivekananda were referred to as 'the saints of Viveka'. Such was the aura of the college that even when the whole university went on strike, Vivekananda continued working; classes were held and to the full strength of its students. Yes, in those days, the colleges would sometimes go on strike for frivolous reasons and work used to come to a standstill. We used to feel miserable from the taunts we received from friends from other colleges for attending classes instead of standing in solidarity with them. Vivekananda did not understand these matters. Did it embarrass us? Yes, it did. And there was also the vicarious desire to take a day off when there was a strike elsewhere. However, the college stood by its values and its way of working.

Vivekananda College had some remarkable professors, each one better than the other in some particular way.

I remember Professor Venkat, who taught us Theory of Automotive Languages—a tough subject. Prof. Venkat, who had returned from the US, was a giver. He was an amazing man, full of energy, and he used to spew wisdom that we used to find difficult to receive. Much of what he said went over my head. He loved to teach and accepted a modest salary compared to what he could have got in the US. He came to India with a clear intention of making a difference, and he was a tough man. He wanted the best out of each of us. Dr Venkat was par excellence in his subject. He spoke to us as if he was waving a magic wand, and we were in awe of him. When he spoke, we used to understand him or seemingly so, for a few minutes later, it was as clear as mud. When he would see that dazed look, he would redo his whole lecture until we understood him. What made him special was that he would repeat it until we all understood him—each one of us. He was also one of my early teachers of 'Ethics in Action'.

Mid-year exams were approaching. This mid-year was about halfway before the semester examination. It was a way to prepare us and have us focus on the exams coming up. The theory part was a bone-crusher. Many, like me, were not confident about the exam, and we were trying to see how we could sit beside someone who knew the answers and who would whisper them into our ears! I hated to walk into an exam hall not being confident. I had never failed in an exam and this was going to be the first, for sure. I was feeling miserable. Most of us were miserable.

On the day of the exam, when we all filed into the classroom, Prof. Venkat quickly distributed the question papers and asked us to turn the question paper face down. He spoke in measured tones, choosing his words and smiling at us all the time. Mathematics was not my forte, but I was determined to give my best. However, this was way over the top. I noticed I was not alone. We were all nervous wrecks. Noticing a little flicker of fear in our eyes, he asked, 'How many of you are not at all ready for the exam today?' A few of us raised our hands, hesitatingly. He said, 'Students sitting in this room, I urge you to resist the temptation to look over your shoulder into another's paper. It challenges my imagination that somebody would have to copy in Mathematics! It is so not done.' Hopes faded in an instant.

Prof. Venkat continued: 'If some of you believe that you are not ready, I will give you another chance. I will reschedule this exam to the next Sunday and we can have the same three-hour exam, but I will have the question papers changed, though. The topics will be the same, but next week would be your last chance. How many of you would want to come in on Sunday for the test?' Oh, what a relief! We could have hugged Prof. Venkat. Only four people took the test that day. He gave no great speech, just a statement, and allowed us to make a choice.

The rest—over forty of us—came in on the following Sunday to write the exam. The exam seemed easy now. The three hours went off in a jiffy. The paper in itself was not difficult. I scribbled my responses in a rush. The problems were solved as if by themselves. Things fell in place and quickly so. I looked around the room. Everyone was at their booklets, scribbling away; intense work that Sunday. At the end of three hours, it was a relief and a lesson too.

The incident left a deep impression on me. Prof. Venkat gave me a second chance. He taught me to be honest. The simple deed of giving and not making a big deal about it was an act of grace. I will always remember Prof. Venkat for this magnanimous act. He taught me an important principle of human endeavour—to give people a chance, a second chance. Catch them doing something right. The Theory of Automotive Language was not that difficult that Sunday. The lesson was not about it at all, I guess.

Over the years, I realized that it is very important to give each other a second chance. We all need a second chance—both as a giver and a receiver. In giving you receive, and in receiving you take the responsibility to pay it forward. Recently, I was cleaning my cupboard and saw my old Mathematics textbook, and out fell a photograph of Prof. Venkat. He had taught us more than just Mathematics. I was in a daze, lost in that nostalgic magic moment.

3

Driving a Lesson in Humility

I was a freshly minted graduate of a leading B-School and wore its stripes proudly on my shoulders. I was going to join a well-known British multinational at one of their plants in Gomia, Bihar. I had been appointed as a management trainee. They chose only the best, yes: I was so full of it, all puffed up with a sense of self-worth beyond compare. My parents were very happy, and my friends envious. The way to get to Gomia was via Calcutta (now known as Kolkata). We lived in Madras (now called Chennai). I reached a day prior to catch a night train from Calcutta that would reach Gomia in the morning. I had received a fancy letter that all arrangements had been made for my arrival and that there would be a car to pick me up from the railway station to take me to the guest house. All very prim and proper, very British. I felt important.

The train from Calcutta was one of those old ones that had seen better days. Perhaps they did not know that I was to board it. It was not even a diesel engine hauling the carriages. I was given a first-class compartment and I was on cloud nine. It was short-lived and lasted till I entered the coupe. Relic is the word. I was tired and soon fell asleep. I woke up early and went to the entrance of the carriage to peek outside, only to get a hail of fine coal ash. The coal-fired engine finally creaked up to the railway station that read 'Gomia', and I got out of the coupe with my canvas hold-all (yes, we had such things in those days). The hold-all was made of canvas, and it could be unrolled into a bed and had large pockets for clothes. I alighted and noticed that there was not a soul in sight to receive me. I felt let down. I heaved the luggage on my shoulder and came to the exit of the railway station. There I saw a nice car, a navy-blue Peugeot, and the driver in khaki shorts and a white tee shirt was walking towards me. Ah, my driver, there he was!

I went up to him and rudely asked him to open the trunk of the car and place my luggage. The driver did not have a cap, and I forgave him for it. He asked me in Hindi who I was, and I introduced myself as the all-important new recruit. How would this man know who he was speaking to! In my most condescending way, I asked him to take me to the guest house. I stopped short of showing him the letter from the company. A diminutive man, he kept smiling all along. He wore spectacles, which was kind of odd for a driver. He said he would be happy to drop me. He walked to the car, bent under the weight of the bag, heaved the luggage in, and almost fell in as well. He then opened the rear door and got me seated and asked me if I was comfortable. This was getting better. Yes, much better.

Throughout the ride, he asked me questions about my family, where I was from, in a kindly sort of way. I responded in monosyllables, irritated with a driver who spoke too much, and in Hindi. He kept smiling. It irritated me no end. But the car was comfortable. The violet plush interiors welcomed a worthy man, I thought. Near the guest house, he alighted, and a couple of the staff ran up to the car and saluted. I did not care to salute back. I thought I saw some exchange with the driver, and they respectfully carried my luggage inside. I waved to the driver. He was a decent man, after all. In turn, the man wished me the best for my new job. The next day was a big day. I was to meet the big daddy of the place—the Chief Executive—Dr S.K. Varma. I was nervous.

I went in early to the factory. The people at the guest house told me that he was a fine man. Dr Varma's secretary ushered me into a corridor that led up to the room and told me that he was ready to meet me. I knocked on the door and walked into the large office. The big man, dressed in overalls, had his back to me as he welcomed me. As he turned around to face me, I recognized. It was the driver from yesterday. I burst out: 'Hey, what are you doing in this office?' It was all confusing, a prank for sure. The 'driver' gave me a broad smile and in chaste English said he was Shiven Varma and invited me to take a seat. I choked and could have died in that instant. My legs had turned to jelly and I was at a loss for words but apologized profusely for my behaviour. He said that he had come to the station to see off a friend. He had seen me looking a bit lost and wanted to be of assistance. He had played along, for he knew I had mistaken him for a driver.

He offered me tea and had a long conversation with me, in the course of which he mentioned that outside of work, one should not be proud of one's education, only use it. As I walked away from his office in a daze, I had learnt the greatest lesson in humility. So, the guest house staff were saluting him, not me! My ego came crashing down, and that day, I lost my imaginary epaulettes and stripes. Shoulders hunched, weighed heavily with lessons learnt, I exited his office.

Humility is about playing a role, any role, sans ego, whatever the role might be. Even if this role were that of a driver. Dr Varma never referred to this incident ever again, not even as an amusing story at a cocktail party. It was as though it never happened. He was unknowingly driving home a lesson in humility.

4

Running up a Lesson in Motivation

It was a cold winter morning of 26 January, very many years ago. I was working at a prestigious MNC of those days in one of their factories in Bihar. The day was special, for this was the day of a mini marathon, all of twenty kilometres. I had woken up at 4.30 a.m. and was present at the factory gate, the starting point of the marathon. It was well-attended and highly competitive. We had to run on undulating hilly terrain, roads that were gently sloping in some parts and steep in others. We were to run to a spot and then return the same way, and the finish line was at the factory gates. There were some really good views all along the road, with beautiful green trees, but who was going to admire them when you were running a race! I was a brand-new management trainee fond of long-distance running. For over twenty years, there had been only one winner for that race—Victor Lakra, a seasoned runner. I was scrawny and a kid in comparison to

Lakra, who was tall and lean, sinewy and well-muscled—every inch a top athlete. He stood out among the crowd of runners; we were over fifty of us. He was confident and had a lot of people milling around him, and he was beaming. A few noticed me and sniggered. I was no match for Lakra for sure.

The race started exactly at 5 a.m., and Lakra was off like a rabbit, with everyone else trotting after him. It was going to be a long race. Unlike Lakra or many other runners, I had no one to cheer me along the way. People barely knew me. I was focused on running. The roads were difficult, and the climbs were torturous and the downhill runs pleasant. Ahead of me by many metres, Lakra was pounding the asphalt rhythmically without breaking into a sweat. Here I was, feeling drained by the cold morning and the sweat of effort. There was no way I could overtake this hulk of a man. All I wanted to do was not lose sight of Lakra. He was my compass and I kept at it to make sure that I was somewhere near him. Then came the final climb to the halfway mark, one of the steepest, the one where you wanted to give up and just hobble. The body kept complaining and wanting to give up. Not so with Lakra, who was lapping it up. He seemed to take big strides with ease. There I was, ready to give up. It was depressing, for sure.

Just then, I heard a voice booming by my side, goading me into action with some pleasantries about the morning—words that I dare not put into print. He was on a bright green Chetak scooter, wearing a brilliant yellow turban and a red shirt, coaxing and bullying me to run and not give up. He did not care that he had had to wake up early to be at a race in which he was not even running. All he did was show up; that too, for someone who was not even in his line of reporting at work. He wanted me to run and give my best. Suddenly, something got into me. I started to run like a man possessed. Now my strides were getting better and longer. The tiredness was abating. I have no idea where I got the reserve of energy. I guess Daljit Singh provided the much-needed words of support to a 'kid' he cared for.

We had reached the halfway mark and people were registering my bib number and waving me away to say that it was done, and I was a bona fide runner! I did not let up and kept running. What was disconcerting was that the forty-five-year-old Lakra was still ahead; he seemed to be running as if it were a walk in the park. I had only one aim—to keep him in my sights and not let the distance between us grow beyond a manageable constant. Lakra did not look back even once. He was his confident self. I felt good, for at the halfway mark, I had just four other runners who were around me, but I knew I could beat them at the finish. The race kept on for what seemed like an endless morning of running.

It was the home run of some fifty metres. Lakra was ahead, and I was tiring. It almost seemed that I was going to lose, after all. Daljit was screaming something. I put some zing into the final kick and ran hell-bent for leather and flashed past Lakra in the final five metres into the ribbon and collapsed in a heap, worn out and tired, with the sweet sweat of success streaming down my face. Lakra patted me on my head and vanished. Daljit came up and, instead of shaking my hand, gave me an affectionate slap on my shoulder. His brimming smile, moustachioed face and twinkling eyes said it all: I had won. The air was full of his loud laughter, and his fists were pumping the air as if he had won!

What does it take for someone to goad another in their hour of need? What motivates the motivator to wake up at 5 a.m. on a cold winter morning? Daljit was one whom everyone would give their right arm to work for. He left an indelible mark on me. As he said once to me: 'Buddy, all you need to do is to show up, just cheer others and help them find their zone, and you will find yours.' Motivation is more about giving than receiving. More about helping another find their edge. A selfless act that can only be returned by paying it forward. That race is still etched in my memory because of a man who taught me the foundation of motivation—Daljit Singh. As for Lakra, I have no recollection other than him patting my head: a graceful man, another great sport.

5

Of a Plywood Plank and Integrity

I held the grand position of Assistant Manager–Administration in an MNC several years ago. In those days, we were rotated through several jobs to give us a good idea about the working of the factory. This job had the perks of being subject to constant bickering and being complained about all the time. It was a nightmare the first few days and I could hardly get any sleep. I was one of the privileged few to get a landline, and yes, it was a big perk in those days. I was to know later that this was a trap, for people would call me day and night. One day, I got so disillusioned that I went up to my reporting manager, the administration head, a wise man, and asked him how he managed to deal with all the complaints so serenely. He smiled and said that one needed to focus on the problem and not the attendant emotions that words carry. Each incident will teach you something, he added. His line of reporting was to the general manager, someone who had hired me just a few months ago.

Cut back to a few months earlier. We were at the campus and it was placement season. There were lots of top companies that came in to recruit fresh talent. A few of us were shortlisted for the final interviews at Calcutta. It was an imposing two-day affair, with a lot of interviews with some very officious leaders. We had lunch in between the interviews. All formal stuff. I was acutely conscious that I was at sea at sit-down luncheons, butlers and all. Helping us through this, we had a kindly gentleman in a navy-blue double-breasted jacket who would speak to us respectfully, asking us if we were comfortable. He escorted us from one meeting to another. He was always available to us, always there with a word of encouragement post each meeting. Finally, a couple of us who were selected were to meet the big boss of the HR function. People held him in awe. Both of us entered an imposing board room in a prestigious building in Calcutta, and whom do we meet? The nice gentleman in the blue jacket. Later, he was appointed as the general manager (GM) of the factory where I was starting my career as Assistant Manager–Administration.

The general manager had asked for me. I was wondering if I had done anything wrong. Panic set in. We were living in a colony in Bihar, a self-contained community, and the company provided accommodation. They also provided some basic requirements, such as furniture and the like. One had to just walk into an apartment. The GM, of course, had a bungalow allotted, which was fully furnished. I was wondering if I had erred on anything. His secretary led me to his room. It was an imposing room, large, with a huge teakwood desk. Behind it was seated the GM.

He appeared to be in some pain, and I asked if all was well with him. He said that he had a bad back. I was wondering if I had anything to do with it! He quickly added that he was under medication. I listened to him, checking to see what he would say next. He said the bed provided for him at his bungalow had springs, and it did not help matters that the bed sagged. He asked me to have a plank laid on the bed so that the mattress would rest on it instead of on the springs, and that way he would have a level bed. That made sense. I told him that I would attend to it forthwith. I ran from the room and into the carpentry division and spoke to the supervisor and asked him to have someone sent to the house to have the problem attended to, and to let me know when it was completed. The time was 2 p.m.

At around 4 p.m., I got a call to say that the job was done. I was brimming with pride, for I had managed to get it done and post haste at that. I would rush to his office and let the GM know that the task was done and with alacrity, and get some much-needed brownie points. I knocked on the door, and he smiled even as he asked me to come in and have a seat. I told him that an 8 mm ply had been fixed and that he should have a good night's rest. He thanked me profusely. I was a tad embarrassed. He said that I was 'efficient'. I was all puffed up. I thanked him and asked him if there was anything else I could be of help with. He asked me if I had done all that was expected of me. I told him that the job was complete and nothing more was needed. He again asked me if I had forgotten anything.

I was at sea and told him that I had done the job. Was there anything else that was expected of me, I asked? He again asked me if I had forgotten anything. I was now getting into a zone of paralysis in my head. Fortunately, he came to my rescue: 'Where is the invoice for the plywood?,' he asked. I told him that I had sent it to the carpentry division and that it was taken care of. He said it was a personal need and that he would have to pay for it. I told him that the bed was a company property, as was the plank, and therefore no invoice was needed, nor was any payment to be made by him. Then, in a fatherly way, he asked me to be seated. He explained that while the bed was company property, the need was personal. He had a bad back and had asked for the plank, and so he would have to pay. He insisted.

I went back to him with an invoice for a princely sum of Rs 25. He paid me on the spot and smiled at me. To me it was the first lesson in integrity as a new Assistant Manager–Administration, something that I have never forgotten to this day: the gold standard of integrity. Thank you, Mr Ganesh Jejurkar.

6

A Rejected Job Offer and Fairness

This was many years ago, when I was a recruiting manager for an MNC and was asked to headhunt for a suitable person to fill a position based in Delhi. It was a difficult assignment and I was really at my wit's end, for the skills were rare in those days. As if that was not enough, my boss said that he was looking for a strong-willed person, a 'people person', a technically strong professional with leadership qualities. Also, he wanted me to look for someone who was strong in marketing or at least had a strong understanding of the marketplace. It was like searching for a needle in a haystack. I had a lot of technical resumés with me, and he wanted a well-rounded personality. Perhaps he was looking for someone who could take over from him at a later point in time.

At last, I managed to locate someone from Bangalore. He was an interesting person, warm and genuine, technically strong and with a good head on his shoulders. The rounds of interviews grew longer, and this was a good sign, as any recruiter would know. We all loved him. He seemed curious, spoke gently; he spoke to all of us with a lot of respect and his telephone calls were laced with grace. I was very happy for I had found the right person. As a follow-up, an offer was made to him. A generous package was called out, and he knew it. In those days, in addition to a good base salary, if one added a car (it was one of the largish Contessas from the Hindustan Motors stable) and a house, it was a great deal. The house was in upmarket Greater Kailash, Delhi, and that was also a plus. We also offered to help him with the admissions to the school of his choice for his children.

I heaved a sigh of relief. He accepted and, given that he was not from the city, I was given the responsibility of giving him a grand tour. Not that I was great at this task, as I was not from Delhi, but I was keen to ensure we made his entry into Delhi comfortable. I received him and his family and took him to the best hotel in Delhi. I told him to rest a bit and that I would come by in the morning and take him, his wife and children for school hunting. My boss, the CEO, was an influential man. He had spoken to a couple of people and the schools were lined up. The candidate was really pleased that there was so much care from the organization. He also met up with a few other senior leaders and took a group photograph with them. Overall, it was a great experience for them. The family thanked us profusely and the prospect left for Bangalore. I called him up later in the evening to ensure all was well. He was, as always, very graceful.

Life was good. He had resigned from his company and I was 'keeping him warm'—making sure that we did not lose him to any other organization. I would make sure I sent him messages and spoke to him once a week. It was a two-month notice period, unusual in those days. One fine morning, my CEO called me to his room. He seemed upset. He asked me about the candidate and if all was well. I told him that all was well and was glowing about my 'personal touch'. It is at this time that he stuck a letter into my hand. It was from the potential hire. As I read the first paragraph, I knew that something was wrong. He started by thanking us profusely for our efforts and said that after much thought and careful consideration, he was regretful that he would not take up our offer. It was like a body blow for us and most disappointing for me.

He said that he had decided to rescind his acceptance for family reasons. His father had suddenly taken unwell and was perhaps on the last leg of his life. He could not take him to Delhi, given his frail health, and with all the family around in Bangalore, he was more tethered to Bangalore. With his father in such a condition, he could not make the move. He was most apologetic and said he could never repay us for our efforts and for the enormous goodness that he experienced. He added that he was enclosing a cheque for rupees thirty thousand to partly compensate for all our expenses incurred with his recruitment. He also added that it could in no way compensate for all the efforts that were taken to onboard him. It could be no restitution for all what we had done for him. Thirty thousand was quite a lot of money in those days. The letter ended on a graceful note, offering to meet us in Bangalore sometime in future and that he could fly to Delhi to meet us to explain his predicament.

My boss was really upset. Such a lot of time had been spent on the candidate. It was a waste of a good six months of search and waiting, and it would be embarrassing as he had also informed the Board about the person's appointment. Despite the setback, my boss was a genuine and practical man. He smiled at me and said 'stuff happens' and that I should start over. He neither shouted at me nor spoke ill of the candidate. He said that the gent was different. He pointed out what was different about the man. My boss wrote back to him to say that while he was disappointed at the decline of the offer, he was most taken with his uprightness and integrity. He said that we would wait for another three months and keep the offer alive and hoped the situation at home improved and that his father would get better. My boss thanked him for the cheque and added that there was no way that he would encash that cheque; on the contrary, he was convinced that this man was the kind of person that the organization needed.

In the end, I did expect the person to show up but he did not. But what showed up was his sense of fairness and character. I could never forget the man. He called me up one day to give us some leads on who could be a suitable candidate and a 'better' person for the job. I thanked him again when we ultimately hired one of the leads provided by him. My boss was pleased with the outcome and did call out the fact that he had 'selected the best'. The candidate stayed in touch with me, and each time he would start the conversation with an apology about his not taking up the offer. A thorough gentleman, he taught me something—what it means to be fair to another. I learnt a lot from him, a candidate who, by his engagement in the process of hiring, left a deep impact on me. I wish I could be like him.

7
Gifts and Return Gifts

Recently, a senior colleague of mine came in from the United States to meet with us. Let me call her Martha. It was a review of work—something I always dread. To explain what I do and have done in the past few months was almost an affront to my sensibilities. Martha was a feisty lady, strong-willed and tough. She had a loud voice and, to top it all, she was a lot taller than me. She had a gentle side too, as I discovered much later. Although I formed an opinion the moment I saw her, when I sat down for the breakfast meeting, I found myself starting to like her. She was warm and caring. She did not speak about work at that meeting. She wanted some help from me to connect with a modestly funded NGO that helped orphaned girl children in Hyderabad. She had come prepared for the visit, having spent a whole day shopping in the US for gifts for these girls. Her goodies included bright combs, hair products, colourful hair pins and clips, some lip balms for cracked lips and lots of warm clothes for the mild winter of Hyderabad. Very thoughtful of her.

Her trip to the orphanage was thrilling, both for her and for many others whom she had invited to accompany her. Martha was eagerly looking forward to the visit. It was the first time she would be at an orphanage. I told her that we called them 'ashrams', meaning sanctuary. The girls in the ashram had never seen a Caucasian. The girls were very excited and did their best to engage her in conversation. Martha was equally moved. They seemed so enthusiastic. Martha sat with the manager to make sure that the gifts she gave were put to good use and for them and them alone. The manager had seen many Marthas. He said that the gifts were theirs to keep and thanked her for her generosity. Martha wanted something more for the girls—a sustainable programme that would give them a decent education, and consequently, a good life. She promised to come again. She gave the girls hope, a vision, a reason to live, and the idea of a life of accomplishment. Very heartening! They all held her hand and would not let go of her. It was a teary parting.

Back to the dreaded reviews! I called the team and we had a half day of nerve-racking reviews of 'how, why and what' of almost anything anyone said. I was plainly tired of it and was feeling very pushed by Martha. She was really tough with all of us. I did understand her point of view. It was a professional need—a review. We just had to live through it, I thought. She made no personal comment, although she was very exacting in her words about what could be done better. I was waiting for all of this to be over. She took the team to lunch and now she was all honey and spice. She had a great way of compartmentalizing things. The team was in a bit of a daze. Was it the same woman who was all fire and brimstone at the meeting?

Later that evening, we were at a working dinner. She excused herself to call up her young son who was in college in the US (it was his morning). She was always worried about him and his studies. He was a clever boy but lazy. In his early twenties, he was a handful for Martha. He was never interested in what was around him or in the community: a loner. Martha spoke to him about her day. She recounted the experience, right from shopping for gifts for the orphans in the US to the time she spent with them and the cheer they shared. Her son was a patient lad. He asked her some questions and perhaps one to do with 'why she had to do all of this at all'. Martha got off the phone and told me about her chat with her son and the calmness that she experienced talking to him.

I asked her about her son. She said that he seemed 'off-colour' but listened patiently. There was something about this call that was different, she said. I asked her if all was well. She did not respond to my question. She did express her worry that he needed to study, as his exams were a couple of days away. I asked Martha not to worry about her son and that he would do well. There was another worry on her mind. She was deeply concerned about Hurricane Sandy that could have struck around the place where she lived. She lived in Florida, a hurricane-prone area. Hurricanes that flattened areas and left people homeless. The thought of a hurricane would worry anyone.

The following day, I met Martha in the morning at the office. She was smiling. She said that she had just got off a call from her son. She had asked him whether he had studied well for his exams. He mentioned quite casually that he had not done any reading at all. He had instead gone to the supermarket and spent over four hours there. He then spent the rest of the day calling his friends, he said. Martha was furious and asked what had kept him away from his studies the whole day. Her son replied that he had been shopping for warm blankets and food for those affected by Hurricane Sandy. He had also formed a group of friends who would help the homeless displaced by the storm.

Martha's eyes were moist. She no longer cared about the exams, she said. The unsaid was that her son had passed the test, the test of what matters in life—values, caring for fellow humans. She had a faraway look in her eyes. The gifts that she had shared with the girls at the ashram had come back to her as return gifts, and how! I understood that look and I smiled too, with moist eyes.

Emotional Intelligence

I've learned that people will forget what you said, people will forget what you did, but people will never forget how you made them feel.

—Maya Angelou

Emotional intelligence is central to the way we move ahead in our life and career. While IQ can get us to the table, it is EQ that helps us sustain our careers. The stories here are personal, and each one of them gives shape to different elements to our personality—whether it is to understand and be aware ourselves, to understand others and be aware of them, or to understand our own motivation as well as that of others. They are stories of anger, emotions, kindness, listening and inner motivation that move us forward. What motivates and drives another and how we can understand where we stand vis-a-vis our own.

Small things matter in life. Like wishing someone on their birthday over a call, not with just a card or a mail. A phone call—something that leaves one feeling happy long after. Small things like listening, and listening to what is not being said, picking up cues. It's not easy, yet with a little bit of effort, one can easily read into what is being said. Mothers do it best, I guess. Besides, I sometimes ask myself, do I understand the source of my motivation? What drives me? What drives others? How can we help both ourselves and others in getting to what they really want to do? When people say something, what do they really mean? Can we understand the nuances? Every event, every incident is a learning, provided we keep an open mind and, of course, a willing heart. EQ is all about that!

1

A Momentary Lapse of Reason

Everything was going well for Bala. He was on top of his job, on top of his game. He was well respected amongst his peers. A rank holder in chartered accountancy, he was very much the first point of contact for anyone who needed to brush up on their skills in accounting. He was ever helping people around and came to be known as a person who was a 'man for all seasons'. He would be onboarded for all new projects and plum assignments. He was always looking for something that could play to his skills. In due course, as much as he was admired, there was a group of people who hated his guts. They saw him as a threat, someone who was always in the limelight and who took away their sheen. While he was aware of what was going on around him, Bala was not politically savvy. He decided to play it by the rules and keep a low profile. Even so, there were a lot of people who disliked him. He could have done something to salvage the situation. Strangely, he helped people and yet was not liked. Jealousy is difficult to deal with.

Not all was right with Bala. He was great at his job, but he was not really good at managing himself, particularly when he was upset. He would say things that could be hurtful, or he would simply 'lose it'. His friends did not much care, as they all knew him well. They would simply walk away saying, 'You are upset and we can catch up later.' He would sulk at his workstation, very quiet.

Bala thought that everyone on his team should be the best and that they needed to work really hard. He did tolerate mistakes of others but would leave the scene of the incident as soon as he could. He took things personally, something that everyone told him to best avoid. He was self-motivated, though. He knew what was happening outside his sphere of influence. But he did not act on anything. He also was not good at receiving feedback from anyone.

A new manager had joined the firm. As part of his induction, he met a number of people of his team. He had a half-hour meeting with each person. The new manager seemed to be a nosey parker and wanted to know about people more than he wanted to know about their work. In particular, he was keen to know about the office and office politics. The team understood the new manager as being different.

At last, Bala was asked to meet him. He knew his new manager had come from a company that was not well known for HR policies, and he did not seem to care about them either. He was known to be competent in his role, though.

Bala was looking forward to the meeting. It was his first with the new manager, and he was confident. However, within minutes the meeting went south. He was being asked questions that did not seem professional, like was he married, whether he had children and so on. Also, partly because was he unprepared for the depth and detail of the discussions. He could have been more prepared, he felt. With every passing question, he felt that he was being judged. What touched him to the quick was when his manager made a snide remark: 'I cannot understand how you were rated as a top performer!' He did not say much. After some insipid conversation that made no difference to him, he quietly left the cabin and returned to his desk.

Bala was a top performer, and here was a manager who questioned his worth. He made a decision that took all of two minutes. He would leave the company, and immediately at that. He could easily get a job. He did not spend time on any farewell events. In fact, he avoided them. He was well-qualified and could easily get a job that paid him handsomely, and he could be promoted too. He met his colleagues and bade them goodbye. He went to his manager and, with an air of arrogance, said that he was moving on. His manager realized that he was still the best employee and did his best to retain him, but he would not listen and said that his decision to move on was final. It was almost as if he had decided not to listen to anyone.

Four years passed. People had all but forgotten Bala. Suddenly, out of the blue, the HR leader from his previous organization called him to wish him on his birthday. He was surprised that despite his leaving the organization, his HR head still remembered him and especially on his birthday. 'How do you like your new place of work?,' the HR head asked. Bala responded honestly that it was not the same in the new place: it did not have an open culture. He missed that in his new organization. Did you make the right decision to move on? Asked the HR leader. After an awkward silence, Bala said that he had resigned in the spur of the moment. A momentary lapse of reason. His ego had been touched to the quick, and he had left in a huff. There was regret in his words. He liked his work, and that was exciting, but the rest of the company was nowhere near the level of his erstwhile organization. 'What did you walk out of and walk into? Was it worth it all?' These were the questions that kept haunting him.

At times, we take actions during a momentary lapse of reason. Something just snaps within us, making it difficult for us to use any logic. Bala admitted that perhaps his new manager had just wanted him to do even better, and he might have misunderstood and overreacted. He had learnt a lesson—and most lessons are not from any university or through formal education, he said; rather, they are lessons from life. So, he, Bala, would not make the same mistake the manager made in his first meeting with his team member. The HR manager was amazed at the depth of the conversation with Bala. A morning well spent on a call with someone who had left the firm. Good learning! All from a call to wish an ex-employee on his birthday.

2

Pauses, Listening and Outcomes

I was newly appointed as a personnel manager at a factory, and I was feeling very powerful in this role. I reported to the general manager. It was a big role that I was handling. I was also told that I was the youngest manager in the country for that multinational company in such a role.

I had my opposite number in the union to deal with. The 'other party', the union leader, was several years senior by age and was known to be a tough man in any negotiation. As I left my room, my colleagues, who were all managers, and who had helped me prepare for the meeting with helpful notes, were standing in the corridor egging me on, telling me to 'teach the guy a lesson'. I was getting all ready for the big battle ahead of me, all puffed up. I could not lose. No way! It was not going to be his day for sure. I had prepared well. I had logic, reason and data to prove my points. My mother, who had seen me readying for work, had noticed I was a tad tense. In a very casual way, she said, 'Just listen more and speak less.' I dismissed it as one of my mother's usual platitudes.

It was expected to be one of those difficult meetings, a showdown for sure. There were arguments for and against. I was all set. I was to meet the external union leader, Mr V. Raja. An external leader meant that he represented several companies as their union leader. He was a legend. He was always surrounded by many people, and he always arrived in an old car that he drove himself. He was dressed in a white shirt, neatly starched and with a fine crease. He wore a dhoti, again white. He had a black fountain pen. At the meeting table, in addition to the usual water, glasses and teacups, there was a pot of Quink ink along with a cloth napkin. Quink was a well-known brand of ink in those days. My secretary, who was a 'covered employee', had placed a bottle of 'royal blue' ink. A covered employee meant that he was technically a workman per law and looked up to Mr Raja as his leader. Sometimes, I wondered if he would ever back me, though I was his reporting boss. Talk about divided loyalties.

My debating skills were going to be tested. It was a long walk to the meeting room. The factory was losing ground, for it was not able to produce the much-required volume per day and of the right quality. Further, we needed automation and installation of new machines. We had far too many non-productive workmen and needed them to be retrained or retrenched. All of which would be opposed by the unions. For some reason, I remembered my mentor who once had said, 'To win an argument, lose your ego; to lose an argument, fuel your ego.' I decided what I needed to do: just walk in with an open mind and a willing heart. I also remembered my mother's advice. I was known to be a good debater and decided to pitch in with my best; I had prepared well. To be a good debater, one needed to take notes and be ready all the time.

After the usual handshakes and 'would you like a cup of coffee' stuff, we dived straight into the matter. It was the union–management settlement discussion for revision of terms and conditions of service for the workmen, which would finally settle into an agreement. I had my own lists ready of my asks from the union that represented the workmen. I had prepared the list, and it was a good one, something that was arrived at after several consultations with the factory managers. As soon as I entered the room, for some strange reason, I decided to pause and listen to the union leader, a man I wanted to 'defeat'. My demeanour changed. I was leaning in, listening, asking questions. He had a point. A good one. I heard myself backing his arguments. He was speaking about the cost-of-living index, the difficulties that were faced by workmen, the situation in the country, the problems with falling production and lack of growth in opportunities in the factory. He spoke of worried workmen and how a stagnant growth could hurt them.

The more I listened, the more I was convinced that he had a good argument there. It touched all the points that I had on my list! The factory had not advanced, and there had been an actual drop in production. The business was weakening. He was gently pushing the management. I shared my concerns about how the workmen needed to stretch and increase productivity and allow for new ways of working with automation and a speeded assembly line. I spoke of marketing and of quality and what it meant to our brand, and how this impacted the business and therefore the workmen. We had to fight the market and not fight each other, said the union leader. Again! It was as though he was reading my script. The marathon meeting ended on a good note, something that would benefit the organization. There would be further deliberations and we would jointly draw up a plan to work out a deal that would rejuvenate the factory. If it meant some voluntary retirement scheme, it could be worked out. He got up and thanked me profusely, as he had expected a fight. It was a longer walk to my office. What if I had not taken a pause to listen? I realized that it was the best thing I had ever done in my career.

My team members at that meeting would perhaps think I had been weak. It did not matter. You don't have to win every argument. It is not about proving a point. Sometimes it is not about winning at all. It is about how we listen, collaborate and work with one another. I realized how much I had gained—and just by listening to another's point of view. This holds true in any debate. For all you know, there would be points of concurrence.

3

Of Satellite Launches and Commitment

A couple of years ago, an incident within the family got me thinking about the whole nature of commitment at work. My wife and I got the news that one of the elders in the family had passed away in Mumbai. It was important for me to be there at the last rites. I was in Chennai and my wife was in Hyderabad, but we both had to be there, for we knew the old lady well: a wonderful person, who had only good things to say about anyone in her life. It was summertime, and the flights were running packed full. The buying of the tickets and the attendant anxieties around getting them kept us on our toes. Finally, we got news of our confirmations, and both of us left for Mumbai. I reached Mumbai first and waited for my wife at the arrival terminal gate. Her flight landed soon after, and we sat in a taxi heading home to my brother's place. It was a very important day for the country. You could even say that it was a red-letter day, for the

Indian Space Research Organisation (ISRO) was scheduled to launch its hundredth satellite. Normally, it would be a news report that I would have casually noted, but for the fact that the younger son of the deceased—let me call him Ravi—was a test engineer at ISRO.

He was one of the key operatives of the satellite launch and had to be at the launch site. It was not one of the complicated launches, but for a test engineer, it was a big deal. He got the news about the passing away of his mother, someone whom he used to dote on. He went to the project manager and spoke about the need to take the day off to attend to the last rites. The manager was a kind man who had seen such things in the past and told him to attend to his family first. Ravi had worked on the project and was quite divided in his mind. He thanked his manager and headed for the airport. His friends had purchased a ticket for him to fly to Mumbai, again not an easy feat. He arrived home, shattered and scattered. He broke down on seeing his lifeless mother. He was inconsolable.

The priest came home to conduct the rituals. As they proceeded, I noticed that Ravi kept looking at his watch. Strange. We left for the cremation ground, and after he performed the last rites for his late mother, we all came home. He insisted on being the first to use the bathroom to shower and asked us to wait. Again, strange. It was a small apartment and had only two bathrooms. We waited. It was the fastest shower time that I had ever known. The first thing he did when he came out was ask us to turn on the television. He then sat in front of the TV and tuned to a channel that showed the launch of the satellite. It had not yet started.

Now the penny dropped. He was looking at his wristwatch to see the time and check if it was the launch time of the satellite. It was his project—the one he had worked on. I noticed a certain ambivalence in him. On the one hand, there was the pain of losing his beloved mother, and on the other, a deep sense of concern for the outcome of the launch. After what seemed like a lifetime, the rocket took off, and while I could understand nothing of what was happening, a news report said that the launch was a success. Ravi heaved a sigh of relief. And why not! He was part of the team that had tested each and every aspect of the rocket that went into space.

Ravi broke into a smile that quickly turned into body-racking sobs that were painful to watch. His brother was by his side and tried to console him. Ravi cried like a child. He calmed down after a few minutes. He was pensive and kept looking at the headlines on the news. I sat by him and held his hand. He said nothing. I did not expect him to. I was lost in my own thoughts. Ravi was an engineering graduate who had been at the top of his class and could have taken any job he wanted. He chose the services. Government employees like Ravi are not really paid big salaries like they get paid in the private sector. They have modest means of earning and living, very different from the world I lived in. What I saw was the sense of commitment, something outstanding. As I thought about this incident, it helped provide answers pertaining to purpose and commitment.

What really motivates people is a sense of purpose. What really drives commitment is a clearly stated goal and the will to succeed. Commitment really comes from within. It depends largely on how you have been wired, how you have been shaped by the environment, how you have risen to the high demands placed on you. In Ravi, I saw the commitment that he drove in himself. I was totally absorbed by what happened. My hand was still in his. It was a privilege, I thought, to hold the hand of one whose commitment to the launch was so high. I am in awe of all the people at ISRO and their leadership team, including the former Director, the late Dr A.P.J. Abdul Kalam (who later took on the role of the President of the country), for instilling a culture of commitment, excellence and pride in so many young minds. They had a deep sense of purpose and patriotism. Ravi had had two mothers to serve: one was his own, and the other, his motherland.

Come to think of it—and the light bulb flashes above my head, comic-book style—perhaps commitment is no rocket science!

4

Lessons in Life and Warm Hugs

Ram met his team member Steven in his cabin in the morning. Steven was a very simple man, highly accomplished in his field, very soft spoken and pleasant. It was unusual for him to seek time to speak to his manager. He seemed self-sufficient in all that he did. Ram offered him a cup of tea, which Steven politely declined. He said that he had already had his cup of tea in the morning. Ram looked at him and saw distress. He did not know how to respond to the pain that he saw in the man's eyes. Steven was a long-time employee and well regarded by one and all. When gently asked as to what the matter was, Steven dropped a bombshell. He said that he had decided to quit the firm. This came out of the blue.

Ram looked at Steven and asked him what the reason was. Steven said that he had got a job in another company that was paying much more, almost double of what he was getting here, and that it would be an elevated role too. Ram saw that he was determined and would not change his mind. He rarely did. Steven was known to be someone who spent a lot of time thinking before he spoke. He was measured in all he did.

Ram was in two minds. He needed Steven, and he also knew that he could not make any counter offer for now. How was he to look for solutions on the fly? He was not sure if it was right to hold back Steven, who was getting a big job in another company and with pay that was double of what he was getting here. Instead of asking him to reconsider and giving him some platitudes about loyalty and that he was a 'company man', he asked him if it was okay if they had tea. The anxiety seemed to abate, and Steven agreed. Ram was just buying time. He was out of aces and he knew it. Tea arrived, and he cursed to himself that the tea arrived so soon. They had in the meantime spoken about the cricket match coming up between India and Australia. Steven had a good knowledge of cricket and seemed to be effusive in his praise of the Indian captain and how it was the best thing that happened to the country. Without seeming to rush things, Ram asked him as to what brought him to his cabin for the chat. Steven said that it would have been easy to send in a mail to him and disappear for the day, but given their relationship, he wanted to let him know in person. Ram knew that the ice was breaking, but not really in his favour. All Steven said he wanted was to bid him goodbye and to see if he could get some advice from him as to how to deal with life and growth within.

Ram was a tough man, not given to a lot of words. Instead, he asked Steven a question: 'What will this change mean to your family?' That was a golden question. Steven calmly explained that it would be a great thing for his family. It would give him the much-needed time with his family and with his wife, who was suffering from depression. Ram did not say anything, but his eyes were asking something more. Steven said that when his wife was unwell, his life's lights dimmed to the point of darkness. He added that when she was out of it, she was the angel in his life. When she was unwell, she would not remember anything. She would sleep most of the day and would sit, tears streaming down her face. Ram was getting uncomfortable about the sensitive and personal information coming his way. He wanted to be empathetic but was not sure if he was good enough.

Steven confided that despite everything, he loved his wife deeply and would go through any trouble just to be with her. He also mentioned that his friends had asked him to perhaps seek a divorce when she was better, and so on. Ram was now clearly out of his depth. He feebly asked Steven how long the condition lasted. About 20 per cent of the time she was in the troubled zone, he was told. This was a bit much. This meant one day in a five-day week. And before he could ask more questions, Steven asked Ram what he needed to do to be a better manager and a human being. Ram was flummoxed! Why would Steven continue to stay with his troubled wife who was not available 20 per cent of the time? And they had children, and he was sure that Stephen was looking after them as well.

He asked Steven how he could bear this inconvenience once every five days. Steven sat back. He smiled and there was a glow on his face for the first time. With a look of joy, he said that for the 80 per cent of the time when she was normal, it was worth every moment. She was very caring and affectionate, an epitome of goodness, someone it was good to be around. She was bubbly and cheerful. She did not want to be depressed. Her medicines sometimes acted up, he said. Steven was rushed in his jumble of adjectives for her. He stumbled, mumbled and stalled momentarily, and stopped grappling for words. He sat quietly. The silence was deafening. He gently added, 'Because I respect her. And I love her.'

It was Ram's turn to be silent. What advice could he give to someone who was so humane? He did what he could do best—he walked up to Steven and gave him a warm hug and held on to him, tears in his eyes. For in that hug, he had just met his teacher!

5
Packing Mother's Suitcase

Mother was staying with me in Hyderabad, and she wanted to go to Madras. Like most octogenarians, she kept repeating what she said—that her suitcase needed to be packed and she wanted my help. I have a code with her. Whenever she repeated herself, I would raise my hand with as many fingers outstretched as the number of times she had repeated herself. I had four fingers up, indicating her score. She muttered that it was impolite of me and reminded me how, when I was a child, I used to say the same thing dozens of times and she would be patient with me. She also chided me, saying that I needed to be reminded, as I had not yet done what she asked. She also thoughtfully reminded me how my firm tolerated me. (I was not going to take that bait for sure.) Clearly she was very excited about travelling back to Madras. Yes, to her it was always Madras, not Chennai. I told her to set aside all the things that she needed—only the essentials, I said—and promised I would pack them as soon as I was back from work. She was happy. I noticed a twinkle in her eyes.

In the evening, I came home to a king-size bed full of clothes and a pile of odds and ends that certainly needed to be discarded, not packed! Why would she want to take her old magazines in her suitcase? She was not going to stay in Chennai forever. And the packets of Meera Shikakai powder (an organic shampoo made from the beans of a special tree) were all over the place. To top it all, she had got these from her beloved Madras! She could always buy it there, I said. There were six bars of laundry soap, and five cakes of bathing soap. And endless sarees. This was going to be a long evening of negotiation. She was a determined woman and someone who could talk you to the ground. I needed to be patient with her and speak softly.

It reminded me of my school days. When packing my bag for school, I used to add a couple of storybooks and stealthily put in a couple of tops (a top was a delightful conical marvel, launched by winding thick string round it and then flicking it to send it spinning off on the ground—a great real-life lesson in physics), a yoyo and a few marbles. My mother would come in to inspect my bag before I charged off to school, and I would be caught. The questions and protestations ensued, ending in a deep sense of hurt surging in me if she put away the yoyo or the marbles and tears shed for good measure. The day she let me carry a storybook to school, I hugged her. She said that I was to read it in the lunch break. All this came rushing to mind. Fast forward: it was the same game all over again, only the roles were reversed. I could see myself smile even as I negotiated with her.

I looked at my mother and tried to persuade her to lose the magazines. Why would she want to carry them when they could be purchased in Madras? I added that the soaps could be purchased in Madras, too. She did not need so many, in any case. She protested that the mags had her favourite stories. I was not sure what to do. She seemed so determined. And my logic seemed to get me nowhere. I was getting irritated, for she was just not giving up. I then thought I would get my wife into the mix and have her conduct the negotiation to cut down the 'unwanted' luggage. Wrong strategy. My wife had had run-ins with her before, and my mother was eyeing her with utter lack of trust. At this point, my wife told her that what she saw in the room was totally insufficient. I think she had some strategy that I could not fathom at the time. All I knew was that my wife was fanning the fires instead of helping me put them out. I suggested to her that she leave the room and I would work it through with my ma.

I knew that a part of negotiation was to use a dilatory or distracting tactic. I used to run these programmes at the workplace. I suggested that we have dinner and then continue the work. She said she was hungry too. We went to the living room. She was happy and spoke to my children affectionately. They loved their grandma, who was always indulgent of their wants, even if they were way out of line. This evening was an instance of this. We avoided pizzas at home, but that day, my mother had no hesitation asking me to order some for dinner. What was irritating was that she said this in front of the children. I thought it was her way of getting back at me. The pizzas arrived in a jiffy and we enjoyed our dinner; the pizzas were delicious. Ma was happy. It was time to get back to the battlefield.

Right then, something stirred within me and made me review the charade that was being played out. Was I going to oppose or would I agree to the 'unrealistic demands' of this lady, bent with age and from the burden of raising three children? And all within the modest means of those times? Was I taking it out on her for the past? Why was I playing the master and the judge? What did I gain from it all? She was looking longingly at me. I relented. After all, what would I tell her? That I would have to pay for the excess baggage? She had carried the baggage of life without a murmur, and she had done it with a smile. I simply put all the stuff in one bag and brought out another one for the remaining odds and ends. I told my mother that I understood that each one of those items was important to her, and I respected that. I looked at her, my thoughts on those faraway days, and instinctively gave her a big hug. There were tears in her eyes.

The bags were packed, the sentiments were not. I turned away and wiped my tears as I left the room. Life is beautiful.

6

Amby Splutters, Stutters and Confidence-Building

Years ago, I had a senior colleague whom I much admired. I shall call him Dr Rajan. A fine man, he was kind to everyone, even his car. He owned an Amby—the good old Ambassador—and used to talk to his car affectionately. Winter mornings were not good for cars in those days. Fiats and Ambys were subject to a lot of ignition trouble in the cold, requiring much coaxing and cajoling. The agonized whining of a car engine in the morning was a regular feature of the times. Many car owners in the neighbourhood would curse the engine, kick the tyres and utter unprintable words. Not Dr Rajan.

Dr Rajan would talk soothingly to his Amby, allow her to splutter, and in all the intervening times would say sweet things to her and 'forgive' her whining. Notice the gender here. To Dr Rajan, the Amby was a 'her'. He kept her in fine condition: well-polished, with clean interiors and a sparkling clean windshield and rear windows. He was always gentle with her. He believed in her and was often heard saying that he knew she could 'overcome the cold winters'. It appeared as if his car came to life after his words of endearment. He used to thank her for coming to life and engage the gears with a lot of care.

He used to give me a ride to work so I went over to his house in the mornings. I was very young then and used to watch him with amusement. If he ever went into a pothole on the road to the factory, he would gently utter a word of apology to her, like to a human. I asked him if it made a difference to his car. He laughed and asked me to try it out with my Vespa scooter, adding that even if I were to kickstart her, I should yet be gentle. I was fascinated with Dr Rajan. I learnt then that a dollop of kindness here and there worked wonders, even with inanimate objects!

Many moons later, I was leading the campus initiatives for my company. I had the opportunity to meet a fine student called Chandra Mohan at a campus in Trichy. He was a brilliant man and a passionate soul—a whiz with anything technical. He had aced the written exams and was shortlisted for the final round of interviews based on his test scores. Just before the interviews, he bumped into me—something I always evaded, for I did not want any bias to creep in, but could not avoid this time around—and started to speak to me. I noticed a lot of stuttering in his speech. He asked if his stutter would come in the way of his selection. I knew that this had its foundation in a lack of confidence and told him that he needed to 'keep his chin up' and do his best, offered some words of encouragement, and ended by saying that he needed to face up to his fears. He told me about himself, and I was confident he would leave a mark wherever he went. He was passionate, intelligent, and caring. I liked him a lot in the short time I spoke to him, and knew we had a winner on our hands. However, I knew that it was going to be tough for the young man in the panel interview, with his minor handicap.

The interviews started, and Mohan seemed nervous and was stuttering a lot. He could not do much, despite my support with nonverbal cues. He was messing up the interview and his candidature was not looking good. The panel members sat in the evening to discuss the finalists and it was a big debate when it came to Mohan. It was a house divided. I guess I got lucky, for I was able to persuade them to clear Mohan. He was put into Sales and Marketing—a killer job for such a person!

Mohan joined us. He was put into sales, and I knew that he was not comfortable at all. His strength was in technology and he would be a fish out of water. To add to his woes, his boss lacked empathy, and for about two years, he silently bore the brunt of the demands that he 'should not stutter'. I knew I could do nothing from afar and always wondered what would happen to Mohan. To cut a long story short, Mohan decided to leave the organization. On his last day at work, he came to me and thanked me. I was most disappointed and, as words of encouragement, I told him to have belief and faith in himself—and that one day he would be a big success. I told him I trusted him and his abilities more than anyone else did, and he thanked me for my words of encouragement. He said he would do his best. He was going to start his own firm, he said. I wished him the best and walked away, really hoping he would do well.

Many years later, Mohan tracked me down and wanted me to come to his office and meet his top team in Chennai. It was in one of the big fancy buildings, with a nice reception area, and was well appointed. He was a hugely successful software entrepreneur and was doing very well in his field. He was very upbeat, very proud of what he and his team had built. When he spoke to his team, he introduced me as someone who worked at a great company and fondly recounted what he had learnt in his first job, the foundation of his success. I was a bit embarrassed and while he was being a good host, I was lost in the wonderment of his accomplishments. I had had no doubts about his capabilities. His team was very passionate and upbeat about the organization. The meeting ended, and I came away feeling on top of the world. What a fantastic story!

What a spoon of self-confidence and self-help can do to oneself! We all need to help ourselves. And we need someone who can be there for us in that hour when support is needed most—someone to help get past that splutter; someone to cajole and coax us, with a gentle touch, to find that confidence in ourselves. I remembered Dr Rajan. This was something that I had learnt from him.

As I sat in my car, it occurred to me that in the time I was with Mohan, something had been very different about him. The stutter had vanished!

7

Photography, Interviewing Skills and Self-Awareness

Many years ago, I had joined a firm led by a passionate entrepreneur, Pradeep. A man of many talents and someone different. Someone you could learn a thing or two from. He used to look for outstanding talent and made it clear that everyone on the team must be someone you wished to work with, even work for some day. I was new to the role as the head of HR, and it was clear to me that I needed help to drive the strategic agenda. There was a lot of work to be done. I needed someone who could be of support to me and as a deputy.

I had scoured all the people around the country, and finally it came down to a couple of people who were not just great professionals, they worked in good companies and had stellar backgrounds. This was something that was important to Pradeep. One of them was from a leading MNC, and I was partial to him. He agreed to meet up with my

CEO, Pradeep. I had a long briefing with him and was preparing him for the interview. It was a delicate situation, as it seemed as if I was rooting for his coming on board. The day of the interview was around the corner.

The candidate was ushered into the office of the big boss. I was in a room not too far, and I was even more nervous than him. An hour later, he came out and I anxiously asked him how it went. He said it was a perfect interview, and I was elated. So, it would be a win for me if he was selected. It would cement my relationship with Pradeep and would be a testimony about my abilities as an HR leader in selecting the right talent.

Part of emotional intelligence is about knowing self and knowing another person well. I was confident about myself, and that meant that I was self-aware and had given myself high marks (read ego). Knowing another was about social awareness, and again here I had given myself high marks. How could I be wrong? I had a long interview with the candidate, and he came with good references and came from a good school. (My hang up with renowned or well-known schools vanished over a period of time, but these were early days, the ones where I was subject to a lot of learning by doing.)

I went to meet the CEO and asked him how it went, smug in the know that it was a no-brainer. Pradeep asked me about the candidate, and I reeled off all his virtues. I ended by saying that he would be right for the firm. Pradeep told me that he had a differing point of view. He asked me if I would like to debate his candidature, given that he felt that he was a reject. He said he did not make the grade. I was speechless. It was as if my world was crashing all around me. I asked him what made him say so. He told me that he was a very good professional and solid in his job. Just that he would not fit our company. I egged him on for something more. He then explained his reasoning.

He had quizzed him about his role and his work and his contributions. The candidate responded confidently. Pradeep was partial to good communication skills and he could find no fault with the candidate. He asked him about his greatest success in a challenging situation, testing out as only a good behavioral interviewer should. All impressive. Pradeep then asked him about his hobbies and the candidate said photography. He then asked him if this was really his passion, and the candidate nodded. He said that photography was his deep-felt passion and something that he was an expert at.

Pradeep then asked the next question, 'What is the relationship between the focal length and aperture of any camera?' This was a fast out-swinger that the candidate could only give a blank look to. He then asked him about his best picture and how he had composed it. Again, the candidate was not very impressive. Many more questions followed, including one about the first camera on the moon. I would have said 'Hasselblad'. That was easy, I thought. Pradeep was relentless. The candidate was out of his depth, and it showed clearly. The last question was about what camera he used. The candidate said, 'Kodak, aim and shoot'. The interview was over.

I argued that just because someone did not respond well to a question on photography, how could he be rejected? Pradeep was calm. He said that in any candidate he looked for three qualities—initiative, drive and passion. He said that the candidate lacked passion. If he said his hobby was photography and that was his passion, he would know a lot more about photography than a casual photographer. I did not give up and asked him as to how he hired me. He then asked me to remember my interview. He was gentle. Asked me to take my time.

Meantime, he ducked down and took out a folio and picked out a paper, an interview sheet that I could recognize. The penny dropped. I remember telling him that I loved reading books. He then asked me the last book that I had read, the ones that made an impact on me, and many more such questions. I recollect responding to him with ease. The books I had read, the latest one, and the authors. It was something that was a passion. It went on to gardening, and again, I was sitting at the edge of my seat responding to the questions. The interview was all about the passion one holds beyond the degrees from great universities and the experience from 'MNCs'.

I returned to my room steeped in thought. It was about passion, not about photography. A lesson well learnt. Look for passion, and drive and energy would follow. A lesson that is still fresh in my mind. Self- awareness can be clouded by the bias we may hold. It certainly did for me.

Career-Building

The best way to predict the future is to create it.

—Abraham Lincoln

Career-building is a whole set of actions starting from an initiative; and the drive to bring out a certain facet of one's self that makes all the difference. Stories of gym instructors who made the cut as the CHROs are waiting to be told. What drives such people?

These are stories of sponsorship, of men and women scaling heights by the dint of their initiative and drive; stories of attitude of conviction, courage and resilience, each one of them impactful and inspiring. They carry subtle messages of how staying grounded plays a big part in our lives. Career-building is also about running a marathon and not just working at sprints and instant gratifications.

Careers are built slowly, often bit by bit, over a period of time. Many things come into play in these moments of advancement. So, what is the magic? How does one get ahead? What is the magic sauce, one would ask? The answer lies within each of us, for we all choose different paths. It's like a great dish made by different cooks. The salt and the water are the same, but the proportions could be different. The differentiators are like the instructions the chef gives, or even the secret ingredient, the unique recipe for a great dish. What does it take to work up a great career? Perhaps they all start with an honest conversation, something that would make a change to the same routine of work, something that would break the pattern. Careers are built by the architects in us. All it needs is a bit of goading, some inspiration, someone who believes in us and taking a chance. Examining our biases and being aware of it. It is also about how caring can be a powerful way to get the best out of people.

1
Of Sinking Cars and Soaring Careers

Many years ago, on a pleasant summer evening, or should I say night, a car careened into the still waters of the Kodaikanal Lake at a hill station in Tamil Nadu. The driver, a resident at the resort, was to take a right turn at the fork in the road that would have taken him into the mountain resort but instead took a left and went down the gravel road and into the lake. Who could one blame? It was all owed to the spirit of Bacchus. The saving grace was that the inebriated driver entered the lake at the shallow end. He managed to get out of the car, a much-sobered man. He ran into the resort and yelled for help.

The sole staff on duty was a gym instructor, Venky, who was at the gym working on his biceps. Venky rushed to the hapless customer, told him not to worry and that he would take care of things. Venky hurried into the kitchen area and got hold of some helpers. He asked the driver to take him to the lake where the car had got stuck in the bog. The red car was easy to spot.

The team worked right through the night to get the car out of the lake. They then pushed the car to a garage that was close by. They woke up the mechanic and persuaded a much reluctant man to work through the rest of the night and have it fully cleaned, serviced and in fine fettle by morning. The car sprang to life. Venky was most pleased, for he had stayed up all night to ensure that the car was ready. At seven in the morning, he went to the customer and handed him the keys to the car, along with a pot of hot coffee, all the while whistling a popular song. The customer was delighted and was raving happy. He had never seen such service ever in his life. He called up the resort manager and conveyed his heartfelt gratitude. He was overwhelmed.

The general manager of HR from the head office was at the resort for his routine rounds. The resort manager told him about Venky, and the GM asked for a staff meeting. Venky was called to that meeting, and he and the helpers were given a spot award. It was a proud moment for all. The GM spoke about the service-oriented attitude of Venky and extolled his sense of values. Later that evening, he met Venky and asked him if he needed anything from him. Venky was quick to respond. 'I owned the problem of the customer, and I need you to own the aspiration of people, Sir,' he said. That was a bit vague and the GM asked Venky to tell him clearly what he wanted. And so it began: a long period of support to Venky, who wanted to 'become someone with gravitas' and not remain a gym instructor.

The GM asked Venky to complete his college education and do a post-graduate degree as well, and encouraged him to keep in touch. More, the GM said he would call him every now and then to check on his progress. Venky was a good student of the time and was quick to learn. The GM, of course, persuaded him to do a programme in HR.

Years passed. The GM went on to join a large conglomerate. Once, he went to another city for some business meeting, and as he alighted from the plane, he saw Venky was there to receive him. He said that he was now in HR in the same organization, although in another company within the business group. Venky was very persuasive. After pulling some strings within the group, the GM managed to get Venky transferred to his own company.

Venky's journey of learning and development continued. He was a man with a positive outlook, born to serve, with a never-say-die attitude. Later, the GM left the company to take on another assignment in another city. By then, Venky had joined a retail company of repute as an assistant manager. The GM never forgot Venky and continued to call him each month and check on his progress, and listened to his reports of steady progress. All very good!

Over the years, the GM lost contact with Venky and knew that he would grow into a very fine professional. One day, out of the blue, there was a familiar voice calling him to seek his good wishes on something important. He was effusive in his praise of the GM and said that he owed his progress to him and never once said about his own contributions to his success. The GM was curious and asked him what the matter was. Venky broke the news that he had been appointed as the chief people officer by a large retail group in India. The GM was on cloud nine. He could not stop speaking about Venky and what he had achieved. What a journey! What a life!

I know this to be true, as many years ago, I was at the resort where Venky had handed the keys of a once-damaged car, now all repaired, to a customer. And a minor detail—I was the GM of human resources who gave Venky that spot award and who had seen the glint of a man primed to succeed. He retrieved the car from the mire, and what was more, he took the time to go back to college. And he applied his learnings.

He is now the CHRO of a very large retail chain. When reminded of his fantastic streak of progress, he shrugged it off, saying he is in debt to the man who drove his car into the lake. It got him to think about what he needed to do in life to lift himself from the bog. What a man!

I guess it all starts at the altar of attitude, with a will to persist, to serve and stay positive in the face of pressure. Something to learn from Venky. Something to learn from sinking cars and soaring careers.

2

A B-School Called Attitude

Years ago, I used to work for a service-industry organization that specialized in hospitality and timeshare. I had quit a very famous British MNC and took a leap of faith to join this relatively unknown organization. It just seemed that it had a great focus on getting the best out of people; a great vision, compellingly sold by the CEO, who was a fine man with great human qualities. He was also a very open and pleasing man. Intuitively, I decided to hitch my future to this organization. It was a learning experience from the get-go. A fantastic organization with an all-pervading positive culture, vibrant and young. You saw eager faces everywhere and all wanting to do something. All they needed was direction. And I was the new HR leader in town. I had all the trappings of someone from a top B-school and perhaps wearing it proudly like a schoolboy for all to see. A rather stupid thing to do, as I realized much later.

My previous company hired the best of people from technology and MBA schools. Even in these portals of knowledge, they would not take anyone less than those at the top of the pile. Secretly, I was happy, for I belonged to that 'club'. The new place had all the right talent, but they were not MBAs. Most of them were graduates, with bachelor's degrees from 'any college', not necessarily the best. Ordinary people. There was, however, something special about all of them: they had an attitude, a winning attitude. The popular saying in the cafeteria was 'Trespassers will be hired'. I was not used to this kind of an environment.

So, what would I do in the new place? I had all the freedom and the authority I needed; I was empowered. I was keen to bring in some really good 'talent' from the leading B-schools to find a way to 'rebuild' the organization. I did not think twice how it would affect the current batch of people. I was too young to even care.

I went to the best B-schools and hired some good MBA grads. It was not easy, as the brand was unknown and it involved 'selling' the brand to them, something that was new to me. In a few months, all of them joined us and the marketing head was very happy that we had the 'right people'.

In a few months, the sales started to go downhill. There was a sense of loss all around. The MBA grads whom I had meticulously brought on board started to quit the company. We had a dynamic business leader. He called for an all-hands meeting and encouraged the salespeople to speak openly about the situation. One of them mentioned that the firm was getting crowded by the MBA types who thought it beneath their 'level' to really sell in the market. It was also something I had noted, and since the salespeople were not MBA-schooled, *they* had been perceived by me to be low performers. An error, I now realized. I was later summoned by the leader and we had a chat.

I owned up to the problem and said that I had not considered what it would do to the team to have so many MBAs in our midst. The business leader was a practical man. In the course of the discussion, quite casually he asked what it would take to build our own 'MBA programme'—something that was a one-of-a-kind learning-and-doing programme, something that would make a difference. I loved the idea. This would be great. I left his office feeling enthused and very foolish for not having thought of it earlier.

We hunted for a good training leader and found Johny Joseph and he built a team of dedicated trainers—Rajsekhar and Munwari Begum. They worked with the rank and file of the team, the managers Kumar, Mark, Mihir, Manoj, Mahesh, Murali, and the field force to find out what they really wanted in such a programme. We made an announcement at the next all-hands meeting that we would have a programme for those who wanted to attend an MBA programme while continuing their regular work. The first 'executive MBA programme', I guess. The programme was called Core Management Skills. It was to be in three phases: Self, Self in Teams and Self in Business. The Self phase would focus on individuals and help them discover their strengths and iron out any career-limiting issues they had. The Self in Teams phase helped them find their feet in working with others and in teams. Self in Business covered finance, marketing, sales and people management. It was presented as an exclusive programme and there were interviews, just to make it feel aspirational to be on the programme. Over the next nine months, we had a programme that covered not just people in sales but those in the resort operations and all other functions, too.

The first graduate batch of the CMS programme was celebrated at a function. The outcome was outstanding. You could feel the engagement, see the sales climbing and their contributions go up several-fold, and things starting to brighten up. There was a feeling of collective winning. At the end of a year, we knew we had a winner on our hands. These programmes were conducted over the weekends, and we had 100 per cent attendance. There was a sense of pride in belonging to the CMS programme. The programme generated a sense of teamwork and shared victories, the aptitude to learn, and an attitude to serve. It grew the realization that the so-called ordinary people were extraordinary men and women who needed to believe in themselves. The programme was transformational for many and the fortunes of many changed, thanks to CMS. I moved on from the organization feeling that my job was done.

Fast forward: I had landed in New York on a cold Friday evening, waiting at the taxi stand. It was windy and I was exhausted. I just wanted to get to the hotel and catch some much-needed sleep. Just then, who do I meet? A CMS grad! I was excited, as was he. He would not hear of me staying at the hotel. One thing led to the other, and by the weekend, a bunch of CMS grads had flown down from various parts of the US, knowing they had someone from their CMS batch! We had a great time that Saturday evening, with much laughter and reminiscing. While the cocktails helped, nostalgia is the greatest high. All of them were doing very well. Some were successful businessmen, and some were vice-presidents (VPs) of large organizations. They had stayed in touch right through. We broke up at two in the morning. It seemed that time had looped back and we were transported back to the time we were at that wonderful organization. We had to break up the party with some persuasion. It was a great weekend of fun.

As I sat in the plane on the long flight home, it occurred to me that this was something magical I had experienced. I learnt that what matters is what we do with what we learn—and it is not from an MBA school education at all. The school of experience and the lessons of attitude matter more than any college credentials. Talent matters—but talent with a winning attitude matters more. Many a time, the most successful have hardly been through the hallowed portals of education. Life gives back to you what you put into it. Much learnt from the graduates I met from the B-school called Attitude.

3

Bamboo Shoots and Promotions

Sometime back, I read an article about bamboo shoots and grass. It spoke about how bamboo takes six years to grow and develops a lot of roots before it shoots up, whereas grass, on the other hand, grows almost instantly. I neither felt the need to watch bamboo shoots grow nor I was keen to see grass quickly growing and spreading.

There was something in the article that took me back in time, to someone who had said the same thing in a different context. Words came rushing back—that experience is a great teacher and lays the foundation of a good professional, and experience takes time. It all came to mind when I read about bamboo.

As far as I can remember, I have always been in a hurry. I wanted to get things done quickly and race to the top, be it in my school days or at the workplace. In fact, in one of my earlier organizations, my boss recognized this trait in me. He repeatedly told me that 'everything takes time'. I thought he was a 'slow guy' and did not pay attention to his words. It was the time of the year for the annual increments and promotions. I was sure I would be promoted. After all, I had done well and deserved a promotion. It was the shock of my life when I did not find my name in the list of promotions. To me, it seemed unfair that a few of my batch mates had risen to the next level, while I was where I had begun. I knew I deserved a promotion, but instead felt unappreciated and not valued. I was sulking, and my friends knew that I was very upset. Even the ones who got promoted did not invite me to their parties, and that got me even more upset. They should have called, and I could have responded that I was 'busy' and not showed up. Now I felt that I was being ignored.

In those days, it was not normal to go ask your boss, 'Why not me?' My manager sensed the question but didn't allow me an opportunity to bring it up. I wanted to resign and 'show him'. But in those days, we did not have the surfeit of opportunities one has today, and I was locked to the organization. He avoided speaking to me on the subject and carried on as if it was another normal day. Today, I know why. Perhaps, he wanted me to understand the value of patience.

The perfect opportunity came his way. As part of an employee engagement programme, I made a recommendation to introduce a suggestion scheme for our 3,000 factory employees. I had a plan: install fifty suggestion boxes at strategic spots across the buildings. My boss was apprehensive and told me, 'Nathan, I don't think this will work. We, as an organization, aren't ready for this.' However, I was eager to prove myself and quite insistent. The project involved an amount of Rs 12,000 (equivalent to over 100,000 rupees today), something my boss rightly questioned. It came down to being a case of my idea versus his 'wisdom', and finally, my idea (read ego) prevailed. I got the go-ahead!

The scheme was launched. I waited through the day with bated breath, expecting tons of suggestions. The first day, I found some coffee poured into the suggestion box that was kept in the cafeteria, and the next day, chewing tobacco wrappers were dropped into it. Six months later, despite good advertisements and publicity, things were no different. The suggestion box scheme was a dismal failure.

I went for a review of the suggestion scheme with my boss and owned up that it was a complete mess. Instead of saying 'I told you so,' he asked me why I thought it had failed. I reiterated his words: we were not ready for it. I had spoken to various departmental heads to figure out the reasons. We concluded that the workers didn't trust the management enough to come forward and offer suggestions. In order to get any suggestions, we had to earn the trust of our people.

We covered the necessary ground to earn that trust after many meetings with small batches of employees, listening to them without any 'management' responses. A year later, when the time was ripe, we launched the same suggestion boxes. This time, the suggestions poured in. My manager called me over and asked me the same question, again. 'Why has it been a success this time around?' I finally understood what he meant by 'things take time'. Sometimes, they just do take time.

Coming back to my position in the organization. I continued to do my work and never asked my boss why he hadn't promoted me in almost seven years despite a high success rate and good increments. I understood that maybe it wasn't yet the right time. It used to bother me but I had left it in his safe hands. Then, one lazy Sunday, he called me to his house. He served me fragrant tea in expensive Noritake porcelain cups. All the time, as I sipped, I was worried that I would be my clumsy self and drop the cup and smash it.

Suddenly he broke it to me. He said I had a new role. It was two levels higher than my current position. It was a pleasant surprise. It had taken too long. 'Let me tell you something about bamboos and grass,' he said. 'Grass grow like weeds, but bamboos take longer, for they take time to grow roots ... then the bamboos shoot up at a rate that will confound many.' He smiled and said, 'I know it's been a long time coming, but I hope it was worth your wait, growing roots. Here's wishing well for you to grow with rapidity.' He toasted me with a cup of fine Darjeeling tea.

It truly was. It was a plum job for a youngster. As I look back and reflect on my career, I do believe that it was better to have waited and worked hard. The promotion did take a while. Worth the wait, though. I would get to rise when I deserved it. I wish I had read the bamboo shoots article early on in my career, to understand better how the long-lasting bamboo takes longer but shoots up high when it starts.

4

Of Marathons and Careers

I have always been fascinated by marathons. In my younger days, I used to do a bit of long-distance running. The more I think about a marathon race, the more I am convinced that it is very similar to how our careers pan out.

In a marathon, there is a start line, a finish line, and a goal to be achieved. How well you perform depends on how well you prepare for the race and how you run that race. When we cross the finish line, when the marathon is over, there is a sense of relief, exhaustion and, of course, celebration. The sheer joy of completing the marathon is akin to achieving a difficult target. And every time, we start to look forward to another marathon—just like we do in our jobs.

The warm-up: As I see it, preparing for a marathon is like preparing for a career. There is a lot of learning, a lot of rigour, lots of discipline and, not the least, a compelling reason to finish. I have also learned that it is important to run the race because you're committed to running it and finishing it, not because you must win. When you join an organization, it's almost like preparing yourself to run a marathon. You complete your education and get ready to begin your career. The skills are in place, the basic selection is over and you are allowed to compete in the marathon.

The start: As the race starts, you can see an apparent commotion and jostling for space, as people try to get ahead of each other—often at the cost of their co-runners. I've seen that the people who've really run a good marathon are people who pace their race well, allow for people to pass by yet keep running. Similarly, in real life, planning and pacing a career is more important than getting a good head-start. A good head-start is important but it is not necessary that you get to the top of the runner line-up. In a marathon, just because someone who started with you is ahead of you by a few hundred metres does not mean that they are going to win the race! And if you're ahead of someone, it again does not mean that you are going to win. It's a long, long race! Our job is but to run the race.

The middle: Here, I remember Daljit Singh—a boss of mine and a wonderful man. While I was running this mini marathon on a crisp winter morning and, owing to exhaustion, wanted to give up somewhere in the middle, he came by on a scooter and exhorted me to keep running and used some gentle words of persuasion—words that I dare not print! I had found renewed energy and started to run. It was a pleasure breasting the tape as the winner. The trophy was special, and all owing to Daljit. He had no need to be there with me. Yet, he came to cheer me on. In your career, you will find a lot of Daljits. Their only intention is to support you, and they do it in a selfless way. I made a promise that day that I would be a Daljit Singh to someone else.

The final leg: The final leg of the marathon is perhaps the most difficult part of the race. Two things happen to you—either you almost give up or you experience a tremendous surge of energy that takes you through. That you are incredibly tired is well understood, and at this crucial point, all that is needed is razor-sharp focus: that you must complete the race. Then you get a resurgence of spirit, and you start over again. You're not distracted by anyone but keep going on and on and on ... and yonder, you see the tape. Others may have already breasted the tape, but it doesn't matter. What matters is that you've now to finish the race. Even as you're huffing and puffing, you realize that you have finally found your own edge, your own winning formula.

The end: When you finish the race, amongst a lot of cheering and applauding, there comes a great sense of satisfaction: 'I have made the marathon.' The marathon is complete because you've achieved your goal. You recognize that completing a marathon is a big part of your life, and when you start to slowly walk back home, your mind is already made up that you will, for sure, run another marathon.

Discovering your true self: A part of our lives is about goals, about how we achieve those goals, and how we move things around it. As we embark upon running a marathon on a cold winter morning, we know that the twenty-six miles three hundred eighty-five yards will take a long time to cover. So will a career—it is really a long-distance race. It tests, among other things, your patience, perseverance and discipline. There is a certain cheer and camaraderie, as there are lots of people running the race. It is very enlivening because it helps you to discover your true self—about who you are as a person.

Just like in a marathon, in real life too, there are highs and lows. Sometimes when you believe that you are too worn out to take another step, someone gently nudges you and says, 'You can!' Discovering yourself in the course of a marathon of a career becomes your ultimate gain.

I love marathons. They help me be human. It is not just about winning but also about how to run the race. I also truly believe that the only person you compete against in a marathon race is your own self. Careers are no different. I hope you too see it this way. We all have different marathons to run. In our own way, we persevere, build skills and prepare for one more.

5

Career Conversations—Honest and Gentle

Ganesh was the best of managers. He was one of a kind, focused and articulate. He could hold you spellbound with his knowledge of PowerPoint slides and excel sheets. He was a true master of his craft.

Ganesh's manager was very bright and accomplished; a seasoned man. Let us call him Narain. He was someone who had more on his plate than others. Besides, he was a regular at parties, for he played the guitar as well. You expected him to be a great leader, and yes, he was. Narain was always surrounded by people, and we used to joke that he had more conversations on his chat window than anyone else in the firm.

Back to Ganesh. They had excellent chemistry between them. They played to each other's strengths and were an awesome team.

Ganesh had been performing his role for a long time, and there came a time when he outgrew his job. Happens. It was time for his yearly appraisal. He had written out a few lines about his accomplishments. He set up a conversation with his manager, Narain. He wanted to be respectful and let him know his current state of mind. They set up a time and place, and the conversation began. As usual, they spoke about anything other than work. Sometimes, to a stranger, it would be strange to see a couple of people speaking about music, art and the like.

Ganesh came to the point quickly. He said that he was not getting anywhere with his current position, and he could not even come by to ask for a promotion, given that the role was not really at the 'next level'. Besides, he was not learning much on his job. Narain, patient man that he was, heard him out and asked for some time and set up another meeting when, he said, he could give some options. The meeting ended with some words of encouragement to Ganesh, urging for a little patience—all very complimentary of his work and sense of balance. Ganesh went off to his workstation with a smile.

The following day, Narain met his reporting manager and outlined a plan for Ganesh. Given his significant exposure to his data skills and his knowledge of excel tools and techniques, they decided that they would look at Ganesh as the next head of a centre of excellence. Something that was aspirational. Ganesh would be happy for sure, they felt.

Narain met Ganesh and popped the question—would he consider being the leader of a centre of excellence for a certain branch of specialization? Ganesh was beside himself with joy. He thanked Narain many times over and said he would give his best and more. In the days following, one could see the difference in Ganesh. He worked like a man possessed. He was always learning, contributing and happy. He spread cheer all around and made sure his team had the best of learning from him. The teacher in him shone bright.

A year later, things were different. Something had happened and Ganesh was not the same any more. Narain, his manager, was at sea about his dip in performance. He was not sure what the issues might be. He knew that there was something brewing at home on Ganesh's personal front, and he did not ask. The business leaders now started to escalate matters to Narain and his reporting manager; this was something new. It was almost as if a star had unexpectedly fallen. Narain decided to have a conversation, and this time around, he asked the simple question: 'All well, I trust?' Ganesh, in a gush of words, explained that he was unhappy due to some personal issues plaguing him and that somewhere he had lost his 'mojo'. Narain heard him out and gently asked him to go back and put some life into his work. He also asked him if he needed any time off in the interim to tide over his personal situation. Ganesh thanked him and said he would do his best.

A month later, Narain was asked to have a 'tough conversation' with Ganesh, as he had not shown any improvement and instead, his team was getting restless. One of them had already quit owing to Ganesh's temperamental nature. In that meeting, Narain heard out Ganesh and was empathetic. However, this time, he said that the firm had given him enough chances and that he would not be able to hold out more. He said that the business had lost their faith and trust in him. Even as he spoke, Narain was not his usual self. Ganesh knew Narain. It must have been very difficult for Narain to say these things to him. Instead of fighting the facts, Ganesh asked Narain if he could help find a good role for him, even outside the firm. Shortly, Ganesh put down his papers. He proposed one of his team members to step into his role. He then went to Narain and asked him how he could be a better manager. They had a long chat.

At the farewell party, Ganesh spoke highly of many in the firm and, in particular, was grateful to Narain. He said that it had changed him forever. Today, Ganesh is a director of HR at a large company. The lead for the job opening came from, yes, Narain. The managers there were so impressed by him that he got a promotion in the first six months of his job. At the year-end review, he was again promoted. His pay saw a hike of nearly 50 per cent. He was also assigned a cabin of his own. All on the back of a great chat at the cafeteria. Keeping one's honesty, giving the bad news and yet being empathetic does help, and how!

6
Performance Evaluation and Evocation

The first performance review is always scary. One is intimidated by it all. I can never forget the first annual review of performance of my work in Imperial Chemical Industries (ICI), a then leading UK-based multinational. The appraiser was my boss, Ravindran G. I was then a management trainee (MT). Nothing much was expected of an MT—or so I thought. I was also not sure what was expected of me and what I had really achieved. The MTs were put through a twelve-month orientation programme, and then we would have some extra months in a few departments. I was working at an explosives factory in the heart of what is now Jharkhand, a state known to have good mines of coal and other mineral ores. The factory supplied industrial-grade explosives to the mines. I was expected to know all the functions and all our customers. I had visited seven departments over the year, working on small projects, observing how they worked and how we could improve, but had not really done anything that stood out. So, when the time for the review came closer, I was quite worried. What had I to show? How would I be received? Besides, one's compensation was tied to the evaluation. To add to my woes, I feared it had not been a great year. I was feeling low.

I was asked to prepare a self-evaluation sheet. I pulled out a form. It asked for a listing of all that I had done. I developed writer's block. I just could not write—not even a few lines. I asked myself if I had done anything at all in my one year. The last date for submission was coming up, and I forced myself to write something. I started to write, and in my heart of hearts, I knew that it really amounted to nothing much.

I had participated in a few events, done a couple of projects and participated in the annual sports events, where I had helped the organizers too. I had met with a lot of people at the cafeteria, workers who thought that I was different, as no one else from the management had thought to have food at 'their' cafeteria, given that there was a 'management' cafeteria as well. However, I could sense the pulse of the place and so, did not lose an opportunity to visit the cafeteria. The mornings were special, as they prepared mouth-watering jalebis, a sweet that 'you can't stop with just one', and kachoris, a savoury fried snack.

Now, how was I to write about this in my self-evaluation?

Also, there were a few other management trainees with whom I would get together and we would have our chats, so I knew what was happening in the factory. Again, nothing I could pen down as an achievement. Yes, I had done some training for the workers, but was nothing to write home about.

Ravindran scheduled a two-hour meeting with me for my review, which didn't make me feel any better. I was totally unprepared about what to say. Why would he take two hours? Would thirty minutes not be sufficient? It would have spared me some of my agony. At the appointed time, he took me in his 'buggy' to the club, which was a stone's throw from the factory where we worked. An unusual place to have a performance review, and I was not sure why he had asked me out. Anyway, we reached the club and ambled over to a table. He pepped me up saying, 'Looking sharp, Nathan,' which meant that I had dressed well. He was smiling. He had a soothing voice and a ready smile. 'Call me Ravi,' he said as we sat down. This didn't look so bad, after all, and I started to feel better. This was going to be easy, hopefully.

Ravi started off by asking me, 'How was the year that's gone by? Do you believe we have lived up to your expectations? What does your conscience tell you?' He was saying, just be honest with yourself. I had been ready for all the questions I might be asked, but now the answers that I had prepared in my head slipped my mind. The two hours meant for my evaluation turned out to be one of the most engaging conversations I have ever had. He kept egging me on with appreciative nods, occasionally stopping me to urge me to sip my coffee, as it was getting cold. I told him about my fear of the evaluation, of my nervousness and about everything I had done over the past year. He never once interrupted me and kept nodding his head; his eyes never left mine. He listened to me raptly. I admitted my failures, mentioned my small wins, owned my goof-ups and discussed my plans. I spoke like one who had no fear of evaluation.

At the end of the two hours, I felt a huge burden had slid off my shoulders. I asked him what I could do better, and he told me in simple words, 'You have done well! Do what you are doing; stay honest and you will go way up ahead. And, by the way, focus on your strengths. Don't worry about what you are not good at. Do small things exceedingly well.' He said he was proud of me and that I should just be easy on myself and not take myself seriously, just the job. He did not speak as much as I did. He was a well-respected man and had a sterling career spanning over twenty-five years.

Ravi said that there would be some great years and some not-so-good ones. It was difficult for anyone to have an outstanding year, year on year, he said. Some ups and some downs were part of the journey. The years that were the 'down' years were the ones that had taught him the most, he said. The most important thing was to focus on becoming a better professional on the upward trajectory of personal growth. As for compensation, it would follow you like your shadow, he added smilingly. Ravi ordered another cup of coffee. He kept up a smiling conversation and asked me to always be courageous and speak up.

We were at the club for almost two-and-a-half hours. We returned to the office and to the humdrum routine of work. What a fabulous time I had had with a man authentic to a fault!

I came out stronger and enriched, with the knowledge that one needs to put in a lot into the job, not focus too much on evaluations and not take them personally. Each time I sit with someone for their review-of-performance session, I ask myself how I could make it more meaningful for them, where I could focus on what has been done, how to evaluate the performance and not the person. I think how not to scare them off but make the evaluation the means to give them developmental feedback and shore up their confidence; to be instrumental and participant in their moment of evocation of their professional and personal growth—just as Ravindran G., my industrial relations manager, did years ago. My hero forever.

7

Payroll Nights and Shining Diamonds

He was a different kind of guy. I met him twenty years ago. I was new to the organization and wanted to come to grips with the organization's issues and opportunities. The human resources department was struggling with a lack of good people ready to work with it. Perhaps it was something to do with the brand. I wanted to check on what could be done, but I did not have enough people who could tell me more. I decided to read all the mails and the dossiers on the desk. It was almost 11 p.m. and I had decided to wind up. I picked up my briefcase—yes, in those days, officegoers had these things called briefcases—and was heading out of my office. We also did not have any work-from-home flexibility then. As I was leaving the office, I saw a light in the corner of the large work bay. Out of curiosity, I walked towards it and heard some humming sounds and a foot tapping. It was music from a tape recorder, and there was this lone guy, printing reams of paper. I introduced myself and asked his name and what he was doing. A mistake, for the music was so loud that we could not hear each other. He stopped the tape recorder. I repeated the question. His name was Mahi and he was printing payroll slips, he said, standing up. Out of respect for my age, I guess. Those days, there was plenty of ostensible respect.

He seemed happy and said that he was doing a very important job. I asked him what was keeping him so happy and why he felt that a simple payroll-slip printing was a 'big job'. Payroll slips were important and had to be done carefully, he said. One extra zero could make someone happy and one zero less would make someone really upset, he said laughingly. He was such a happy guy, with a great attitude. It was already late, and I did not want to disturb him. I told him that perhaps we should be meeting up the following day. He was cheery and said that he would be available at 10 a.m. in my office. He had said that it was very important to ensure quality, and he was checking everything. It was difficult to ignore this guy. He enjoyed doing what he was doing. Moreover, he was passionate about doing it right. He had a sense of humour. My impression about him was warming as he took me through some details. His excellence in his work was shining through. He had a glint in his eye. He looked confident. I started to like this chap. I left the place deep in thought. Excellence is all around you, if you choose to be aware of it.

The next day at ten, there was a knock and the young man was at the door. I invited him in and asked for some coffee for the two of us. I told him I was the new general manager–HR and that I was curious about many things in the office. I then asked him about his background. He said he had done his MBA from a business school that I had never heard of. I made a jocular reference to that and expected him to react. He simply laughed and said that the B-school closed down after a year of operation. He was from the first and last batch—again he laughed. I winced. This was not going right. For me, someone from a tier-three institute, and arrogant at that, was difficult to absorb. A one-year programme was all he had. He said he had graduated in history.

My impression of him was heading south. Normally, I would not ask for his grade point index. I will never forget this—forty-eight per cent, he said. Third class, he added with a smile. He said he was glad his college days were over. I had always been on top of my class, and I had a certain view for those who had low scholastic scores.

However, he had a great attitude.

Just then our Regional Manager–West called me and began pounding me for not finding a right HR lead for the West region. I told him I had found such a person, and that he was my right-hand man. He was my best and had to be empowered, I added. Sanjay, the regional manager, was most happy. He said that he would be supportive.

I then looked at our payroll gentleman and asked him if he was willing to go to Mumbai as the region's HR head. 'Happy to,' he said, adding that he never said no to any job. He did point out to me that this level was three levels above his current one and asked if I was 'confident' putting him in the role. I told him that I had every confidence in him.

Over time, Mahi turned out to be a winner all the way. He was voted the best HR manager time and again. I had the privilege to be working with him for a few years, and then he left. He grew rapidly in a short period of time. He went on to become an HR director in a larger MNC.

His mantra: 'Stay positive, be passionate at work, never miss an opportunity, and stay ahead of the game—always.'

He called me recently to let me know that he was going to some faraway fun place—Hawaii. He had been chosen as one of the top 1 per cent of performers at one of the top US computer firms. I forgot all about his background and his third-class marks in college.

You can never put a good man down. What a diamond! We don't much care which mine shaft the diamond came from or its pedigree. Diamonds sparkle in the darkest nights and in the brightest of times. Diamonds are diamonds. Forever!

8

Career Setbacks and Renewal

Irfan was a serious professional, had a cushy job and a premier club membership. Life was good. There was one thing that was missing. Happiness. He was the happiest when he was home. He had his twin daughters to dote on and play with, and had fun doing small things for his beloved wife, Zahira. On the other hand, his happiness quotient at the office was almost at the bottom of the scale. He had a boss who was always finding fault, wasn't appreciative and was never satisfied with anything he did. He would receive words of encouragement from many in the organization but never from his boss. It was almost as if he had sworn never to catch him doing anything right. Worse, the boss wanted people in the leadership of the firm to form themselves in his own image! Irfan was not happy at all. He would break into a smile each time he sat in his car, heading home. He would drive into a world of joy. Sometimes at night, when he switched off the light before he hit the pillow, he thought he 'lived in a land of two shadows'.

Zahira, his wife, was a simple, happy-go-lucky woman to whom happiness was what one made of life. She was a postgraduate in computer science and had chosen the role of a homemaker. She was not unhappy with her decision. She had been working in an IT company and had been doing well. When the twins were born, she decided to take a break. She missed her office, and they missed her too. They would call her at least once a month to enquire about her, and it was well understood that this was more of an invitation to her to come back to work. Zahira was a calm woman. She was always polite and responded with a promise of 'soon', accompanied by her infectious laugh. Everyone who called her also knew that she would return only when she wanted to. The calls were more to ensure that she did not go to any other company. All a nice game of enticement, but Zahira held the aces. Irfan had seen these calls and was always in wonderment at the grace and panache with which she handled them. The curious part was that she never came to him for any advice. She seemed to be fairly clear about what she wanted.

One day, when he came back from his office, he was surprised when his wife asked him to quit. She was really clear and told him that there was no point in being unhappy, living in a toxic environment and being sad with life. The money and the perks could wait, she said. To Irfan, this was a big decision. They had a long conversation. She asked him to write a list of what he got out of the job that made him happy and what made him unhappy; this could help him decide. Irfan did not even have to write anything down, as he had already made up his mind. He quit his job. This was when he did not even have another job in hand. When his friends heard of it, they were astonished and said that it was not a very smart thing to do. Irfan was not bothered. His company tried to retain him, but he was firm. Enticements of increased compensation made no difference to him.

Irfan spent much of his time asking himself what he was good at and what he loved doing the most. He started to write a diary in which he documented his thoughts. He took the feedback of friends and ex-colleagues. He did not feel judged, nor did he feel stressed with his feedback. He became a lot calmer; he also noticed that his twins had started to come up to his side and talk to him whenever they could. They were always hanging about near him.

He also took feedback from friends and colleagues about what they thought he did *not* enjoy doing. He learnt a lot about himself, including his dark side. He could now look at himself in the mirror and feel fine. He started to do some physical exercises and was also growing in confidence. The stress at work had led him to take pills for blood pressure. His doctor said that he did not need them now; he was getting better. He went on long walks, listened to music and learned to cook. He even took his family on a short holiday to a nearby place; not expensive, but some place away from the city. It was one of their happiest times.

He felt that it was time for him to return to work. He started to write out a resumé. He was not sure how he would explain his two months of unemployment. He decided that he should not feel stressed and would simply state that he had taken time to rejuvenate. There were several interviews from companies both large and small. He decided that he would research them first and interview them instead of just them interviewing him. It works both ways, he felt. A couple of months later, he found a good job, though not all that high-paying; the brand was not as well-known, either. He did not care. He liked the person who interviewed him—yes, such things happen! Irfan had asked to meet a couple of people who would be his colleagues, and he did. They seemed so stress-free! He felt that coming here was the right decision to make.

There was no looking back. He could now laugh at silly jokes and not stress about work. He had found his edge, and his happiness. The firm loved him too. All this was because he had had the courage to answer some simple questions: What do you want of life? What does this job mean to you? And, ultimately, it was all thanks to a simple woman who asked some simple, deep questions—his wonderful wife.

Culture-Building

If you want to walk fast, walk alone. But, if you want to walk far, walk together.

—Ratan Tata

Culture is all about values in action. How do we preserve consistency between saying and doing and make sure it stays on course? What do people hear when they listen to one speak? What do they see when they look into the speaker? Do they see integrity in action? This section also takes a look at how that culture shapes policies. How do we develop small habits? Do we believe in the good truth, or little lies? These are interesting stories of humility and purpose.

Culture is about what people do and what they are driven by. What they stand for is about the culture that defines them and their environment. Many a time, we ask ourselves what our real purpose is. Partly, culture is also about empathy that works actions of the biggest of CEOs who know what it is to live the hard times, who take a moment to live the life that is so extraordinary to those who are less privileged. The funny part is that culture is not written on a piece of paper. It is always experienced. As they say, it is 'the smell of the place'. And as is said—'Culture is about what you do when no one is looking'.

1

Integrity in a Bottle of Water

Sometimes, leadership is in not speaking about it. It is in simple acts that speak louder than words. I was in the chairman's office for a short meeting. I had gone there well prepared. Sumesh, our leader, was a simple man and well-grounded. He was generous to a fault and well-respected by all of us, and he had a huge reputation in the community as well. He had a broad smile on his face most of the time. It was difficult to catch him looking upset. He liked meeting people and having long debates around subjects that ranged from work philosophies, the disparity of opportunities for people to, of course, his own subject of expertise—audits and accounting.

Most meetings with him started off as being short ones, but they gathered a life of their own. Sumesh started speaking about the life of young professionals and what was expected of them in today's world. This was one subject that could take hours. I was getting impatient, as I had some urgent work pending, but how could I tell the big man that I was in a hurry? It so happened that he got a phone call; normally, he would not allow a phone to distract him. I guess it was a blessing for me when he picked it up. He spoke briefly into it and put the phone down. He said that he had another meeting to attend and asked to be excused. I could have hugged him for it. We were preparing to leave his office, and I was all smiles. Saved by a phone call.

Just then, a new recruit came into the room unannounced. He went up to the chairman and introduced himself and said that he had joined a day ago. Sumesh did something extraordinary. He asked him to be seated and showed no signs of any hurry. He asked about his settling down and asked him to reach him in case he had any issues. The whole conversation was devoid of any sense of haste.

At around 7 p.m., the chairman's driver came into the room to help him with his heavy briefcase and a small box of files to be taken to his car. The driver pocketed a bottle of water from his desk and was headed to the door when Sumesh asked him to put the bottled water back. He said that it was company property and could not be taken outside the room. The driver protested, saying that it was an inexpensive bottle of water. He added that he was moving to another official meeting after all. Sumesh would not hear of it and asked him to put it back. He could always buy another bottle on the way to the meeting. He said that whatever belonged to the firm must not be taken outside the office. The driver shrugged his shoulders and walked away.

I was watching this whole scene play out in front of me. What a lesson in ethics! No big advice or pontification. The everyday leader sharing his values in a subliminal way—something that was not lost on the newcomer and me, of course! Sumesh never referred to this incident in his talks. It was something I will cherish for life. The standards of ethics were of such a high level that it needed no rule book to tell us how ethics were to be practiced. We had just witnessed a gold-standard leader in action.

2

Little Lies and Life

Growing up, my mother told me to avoid telling lies. Like all mothers, she was keen to get the right culture training in her children. I never thought much about it. There were lies, big ones and little ones. Life moved on and I did not think much about it. I had moved to a few cities to live and work. Now I was in Hyderabad, a wonderful city. I loved it. It was very welcoming, with no pretensions, and culturally vibrant. Hyderabad boasts of some of the great monuments of the country.

As my induction happened early, I took advantage of the time and visited a number of places in the city. Each day was a new experience; the Hyderabadis were such wonderful people. I moved into a house which had a small patch of green around it. Everything was blissful.

My mother lived in Chennai, the great city where I grew up. My mother was growing old, and I invited her to stay with us in Hyderabad. She was very reluctant. The only way to persuade her was to tell her that she needed to move because it would make her grandchildren happy. A good gambit: it worked. She came home, and when she saw the greenery around the house, she smiled.

Then she took over, called the gardener and told him what she wanted were flowers and herbs. It was out of my hands. She was like that, taking charge of things. She also loved to watch the inane serials on TV. She loved her grandchildren, doting on them and spoiling them silly. She told them stories, myths and tales of yore. They were fascinated by her engagement. This was her own way of passing on the baton of beliefs, seamlessly seeding cultural and ethical values in the children.

One day, she looked at me and, in front of my kids, asked me if I always spoke the truth. That was a tricky one. The children were looking at me eagerly for a response. I mumbled that I always spoke the truth—well most times, and turned away. She told me that I should always be truthful. Even little lies should be avoided. An embarrassed me ran from the room, vowing I would never meet her in front of my children during her storytelling times. I could never tell what she would come up with next.

It happened quite innocently one day when I was returning from a business trip. My wife asked me what time I would be coming home, and I told her that I would be there around 10 p.m. I did not tell her that I was actually catching an earlier flight and would be home a couple of hours earlier. I wanted to surprise her and uttered a 'little lie' about the time I would be home. Guess what happened! My flight got delayed and I got home only at 10 p.m. So, in the end, to my own cost, my little lie turned in to truth. This was crazy! It was as if my mother had some special influence.

A couple of days later, I went to the grocery store, and my wife phoned to ask me if they had sweet potatoes. I had seen them on display, but I gently said that they were out of stock. A little lie. I would finish the rest of my purchases in the shop, and then I would surprise her by bringing home the sweet potatoes, I thought. I finished shopping and went to the vegetable section where I had seen the sweet potatoes.

To my surprise, I found that they were missing from the shelves. They were all gone. All in thirty minutes. It could not be true, I thought. This was the second incident in a week. I was feeling silly. I shrugged it off and told myself that I should not let my mother's pontification get under my skin.

The following day, my wife asked me if I was going to start visiting the gym again, since the traffic had eased. It was her own way of gently nudging me to work out. I was also thinking of going to the gym. There is always a starting trouble in such things. The spirit was willing but the legs were like lead. Clear signs that I was feeling lazy and my heart was not in it. I went to the car and then returned and told her that the car would not start. A little lie. She didn't give up and made it a point to speak to me when my mother was around. It was two against one and so, with tail between my legs, I sheepishly said that I would return in an hour. I went to the garage to take out the car and found that two of the tires were punctured, and there was no way I could be driving for some time now, let alone going to the gym. Now the little lie game was getting a bit too much!

Perhaps there was a bit of truth in the lie game. At a subconscious level, it starts to play out what the conscious lied about. I was living the lie! It was time to stop. I told myself that it would be so much better to avoid these little lies. My mother was in her room, reading a book. I went up to her and gave her a gentle hug. She was a bit taken aback. She was not used to unsolicited acts of affection. I smiled and told her that she was right about the 'little lies'. Best to avoid them. It is better to speak the truth and pay the price—reap the rewards of being at peace with oneself. I told her that I was leaving for Mumbai the next day. I sat in the car and headed to the airport and gave a call to my wife. She asked me when I would be back. I told her truthfully that it would be the day after and smiled. Life is more beautiful without lies, even little lies.

3

Of Purpose and Job Satisfaction

I was in Bangalore to watch a cricket match. This one was special. We have a yearly event called 'Impact Day', when employees commit to devote the day to serving the community. The day is sponsored by the firm. I was part of a thread that focused on specially abled children. The team had decided to bring some cheer to the children with a cricket match.

The rules were clear: we would field players who had never played cricket, and yes, we would play fair. I knew how to play the game, so I was relegated to the ranks of the spectators. Most of our team was made up of a motley group of men and women who did not even know how to hold a cricket bat. The opposing team was made up of players who were mostly below the age of ten and who perhaps knew the game a lot more. The cricket ground was an open ground next to a construction site. The wickets were three sticks that were fixed into the ground.

We did not have many adult spectators, as most of the employees had been called up for duty for their own threads. It was a well-contested match and was attended by a large contingent of unruly children who were not even sure of the rules of the game but were applauding when it seemed appropriate. A few teachers were around to keep some of the restive children in check, lest they wandered over to the pitch. The rest of the spectators, the few of us, were office-goers on a late Friday afternoon, enjoying the game. We were clearly on the back foot here. These kids were good and they were so happy. They had got away from the classroom for a couple of hours to play with us. We all had a great time. We were getting beaten hollow, and everyone was laughing and having a rollicking time. Funny, we were happy getting thrashed by children. I had changed my loyalties and was openly supporting the children against our team. Cricket is an emotional game, they say.

A young lady came and sat next to me and introduced herself. Said she was Moumita Banerjee, and that everyone called her Mom. Yes, that was her name. She ran a bridge school programme that prepared the children of migrant workers so they were 'ready' for mainstream school. I asked her what she was doing at this institution and what her story was. Mom said that she was once working in a large multinational company in a comfortable job. She was on the fifth floor of a nice new building that overlooked a vacant plot of land. It was a great view, and she saw a lot of construction activity around her campus. She had not paid attention initially, but one day she noticed that the migrant workers had built a lot of small shanties along the boundary. They were all migrant workers from other parts of India. She also noticed that every day, lots of children wandered about aimlessly, playing or caring for their younger siblings. It occurred to her that the workers had no access to education for their children. So, almost over a thousand of such children in the vast stretch of construction were sans education and pretty much played around the whole day or were employed as rag pickers. A condescending way to put it.

Mom could not come to terms with herself and decided that the children needed an education. She quit her well-paying job and started a preparatory school where children could catch up on the learning they had missed and then go to normal schools. So, Mom and a bunch of her friends and teachers now work to 'bridge the schooling of three years into one' and cross the gulf that kept them from being in a class of children their age. For example, eight-year-olds could enrol in grade three instead of starting school in kindergarten. This meant teaching them for over eight hours a day, motivating them to come to learn, and getting their parents to recognize that they would have to pay for normal schooling. Very difficult indeed. It asked for a lot of commitment from Mom and her teachers. As I was listening to her, I was fascinated by her passion and zeal in her work. She had to network with non-government organizations (NGOs) and other organizations to seek funds, train teachers, organize health camps and motivate parents to continue sending children to school.

She said when she quit her job, she faced a lot of opposition and entreaties by her firm. They said they would raise her salary and would do anything to keep her. She told her manager that she would come back one day and when she asked for help, would she get their support for her venture. Her manager, a wonderful leader, promised all help. Moumita went to an NGO as an unpaid trainee to understand how it worked. She was in a hurry and wanted to learn as much as she could as fast as she could. She did not stay there long.

She met with a few friends, who all thought she was silly and 'had lost it'. She had all of two helpers and started a small one-room school. She had persuaded the construction owner to help her keep the children, else they were a hazard at the site. Also, their parents would be happy that they had a 'creche school'. The one room was not enough and soon, they had more than one room. The construction team built a small temporary shed for the school.

Why would a well-paid young executive give up everything to do such a thing? Meanwhile, the cricket match was in full swing. I was completely absorbed in what Mom was saying. I automatically clapped my hands when I heard someone applaud. I asked her what motivated her to give up everything to plunge into such work with long hours, worries about funding and little appreciation. Where did she derive her job satisfaction? Just then, a little girl came up, and Mom bent down to listen to her. The child told her that she wanted to go back to her prep school instead of wasting her time watching the cricket match. Would her teachers teach them some more time in the afternoon, so that she could 'quickly' go to a regular school? Mom looked at me and smiled.

I got my answer in her smile. As I walked away from her, I understood the meaning of purpose and what satisfaction meant to a selfless leader. Mom, you live up to your name. You do!

4

Promises Made and Promises Kept

It was one of those moments that Vincent feared—a difficult conversation. This was with a manager, a good woman of great potential and someone well-respected in the company. Priya was ready for the role, and he had wanted to promote her to head a small unit. He had proposed her name for promotion and patiently taken up the matter, laying out all her strengths and why she was suited to the role. It had been a long conversation with the business leader, who had not been supportive. In the end, he agreed after a lot of persuasion. Now, with the thumbs-up from the leader, he had called her and told her that she would be taking on this assignment. An announcement was going to be made.

However, just a day before the announcement, the business leader, Vincent's boss, backed off saying she did not have the requisite skills and strength to take on the assignment. Simply put, the deal was off. Vincent was not happy with the outcome.

Priya had been with the firm for over five years. She was a good employee and had grown steadily. She enjoyed the trust of her leaders. She had a small team. They all loved her for her straightforwardness and calm in all that she did. She had a soothing voice and was pleasant of disposition. She was a good listener and someone who would keep confidences and was the go-to person for all delicate and sensitive matters. At the same time, she had strong views that she shared openly and fearlessly. She was someone you wanted on your team. Vincent, her reporting manager, was fond of her as a good professional. She was reliable. What she lacked was visibility to the leadership: she was capable but did not promote herself.

Vincent had to break the bad news to her. He would have to tell her that her promotion was not going to happen. He had to eat his words. He called Priya to his office. It was not something that he enjoyed, having this kind of a chat. It called to fore his own position and was a reflection of his lack of influence. It was not easy on him. He broke the news gently to her. It was a huge shock for her. She asked if she lacked the qualifications or experience. She said that based on the discussions, she had told her family and that they would be devastated. She was not happy, and she suddenly turned quiet. All his words fell on deaf ears. Suddenly, she said that she had decided to quit the firm. It was all over. She would find another place that respected and honoured a leader's word. That hurt! Vincent kept the conversation going. He was empathetic and got her to keep speaking.

Priya kept talking and it seemed that she had said everything she had on her mind. She said that the whole deal was poorly handled. Vincent tried to make the conversation optimistic. He ended by saying that it was a promise that he had broken and was sorry for it. He said he would make amends; a weak statement, he felt. Priya could see that her manager was sincere. Before she left the room, he asked her to reconsider her decision. She was clearly flustered and said she would rethink her decision about quitting the firm. She left the room, but the shadow of a bitter conversation hung heavy.

Vincent was worried that she would leave the firm as she was deeply hurt. He had two options: either to give up and take her resignation as fait accompli and wait for a resignation mail to reach him. The other option was to find a way to ensure there was enough support for her candidacy as a manager. He spent time with her colleagues and learnt that she was balanced and diligent. He gave her some small projects so that she would get some visibility among her peers and the leaders around her. His colleagues were surprised with his sponsorship of her candidature. Priya was also surprised at the change she was experiencing at work. She was invited to important meetings and her opinion was sought. Some of the reports that were to go the leadership were routed through her, and she was asked to review them before they were submitted. It was all very strange.

Vincent did not immediately try to find a role for her as a manager. He spent time with the business leader and tried to find the areas that Priya needed to work on and shore up. It took a year and some coaching. He could see that she had developed into a good leader. Now to find a good role for her. It was time for a review of performance, and at that meeting, Priya's name came up strongly. A role had opened up where she could fit. He was a lot wiser this time. He spoke to her of the opportunity and made her go through a couple of mock interviews. He prepared her for the role. The time came for her to attend the final interview for the position. Priya was confident. There were endless questions, and she cleared them with aplomb—not surprising at all. The panel was convinced of her competence and leadership. She had won.

Now, it was his turn to call her to give her the good news. It was a short meeting. He congratulated her and told her that she would be heading a new business unit. Circumstances had changed. He complimented her on her patience and faith in the company. Vincent did not say much. Priya was super happy. They both smiled and shook hands. His thoughts lingered long after she had left, and for good reason. Vincent had had good mentors, one of whom had said, 'Life is not about just making promises, it is more about keeping those promises. People watch your actions, not your words.' Sometimes, it is also about the little promises that are made and the effort taken to deliver on them. It builds trust and lays the foundation of a good, solid culture.

5

Between Saying and Doing—Living the Hard Times

Peter was no ordinary leader. He was the CEO of a large multinational, someone who had everything at his beck and call. He was a well-known professional, sincere and very hard working. He had a great vision for the firm and worked to get his team aligned to his vision. He also lived a good life, and private jets were not alien to his travels. He dressed well and paid attention to the smallest details when it had to do with his attire. The finest suits and shirts, nothing but the best of shoes and accessories, right down to the exclusive gold Montblanc pen in his inside breast pocket. He had identified India as a country for his firm to grow and was involved in outsourcing before others had even thought of it. He visited his establishments in India at least twice a year. His focus on growing India was unshakeable. Then came the downturn of 2008. I remember this as if it were yesterday. The economy was crumbling, and it was a difficult time all around.

Peter was coming in to meet his troops, something that he did all over the world, given that he was the global head. It so happened that I was deputed to manage his India trip: stressful, to say the least. I had never handled such an assignment, and I had to make sure that it went off well. I had gone over the detailed plan many times. He was very picky about where he stayed and what car was used. He was also particular about the driver, and even the small details about what he ate for breakfast were mailed to me by his thoughtful assistant from the US office. I knew, for instance, that he was lactose intolerant. I also was aware that he was allergic to mushrooms and nuts. I had done my homework. I knew more about his dietary preferences and dislikes than of my own family. The magical day arrived, and I was all set.

I woke up early in the morning and went through the details of the plan one more time. The plane was going to arrive in the evening. Not in the morning as in the past, when he had come in a private jet. This was in one of the airlines that the firm preferred, and the plane was landing in the evening. I went in early and had a large European car readied for him at the airport. I was in my Sunday best and had shined my shoes to a mirror finish. All ready for Peter, our CEO.

When I received him, he was the same cheerful man that I had known him to be. The European car and the driver (in his best white uniform) came right up to the kerb the moment he came out of the airport gate. I was sure he would be impressed. I had met him on my past visit, and there was a glint of recognition. I introduced myself. The first thing he asked me was if there was a yellow-top cab available. Those were not the days of Uber, or he would have asked for that. I said that it would take a long time to get one and so, perhaps we should use the hired cab. He insisted on putting his luggage in the trunk on his own and sat in the car. The visit was off to a bad start. He was tired but kept a pleasant smile for me. It was difficult for me, and I was tied up in a knot of anxiety. He gently told me to stop the big car for his visit the next day to the office. I was in a quandary. He could see it in my eyes. He suggested thoughtfully that he could ride in my car to work and I could pick him up from the hotel. This was even worse! Now, how could I tell him that I had but a modest car! The drive to the hotel will be a long one for me.

The following morning, I cleaned my car twice over and reached his hotel. He was really graceful. He sat in the front seat beside me and had many questions, many of which were about what was happening in India. I was not even sure about what he wanted and why he was asking these questions. I was hoping we would reach the office at the soonest. We finally got there. The India CEO was waiting for us. He had asked me if I wanted to trade my car with his for the hotel pick-up, for he had a bigger car. I had decided to stick with my own.

Peter was perfectly at ease with the people he met. We had organized a townhall, where Peter made a presentation and communicated the vision for the firm, the state of the economy and the plan for the firm. The townhall was a great success. He asked us to be focused on work and conscious about cost. Many questions were raised, and he answered all of them in an honest and disarming way. He gestured a lot with his hands, and that was when I noticed something—he was not wearing his gold Rolex; instead, he had an obscure watch! The gold Montblanc was also missing. The black crocodile leather briefcase was missing, too. The meeting ended, and we made the short ride to the hotel.

Peter asked me about the townhall and if he had answered all the questions and how they were received. I told him that the audience loved his answers and that his optimism was infectious. Gingerly, I checked with him if I could ask him a question. He smiled and nodded. I asked why he was not wearing the gold Rolex and instead had a normal digital Swatch. He smiled and responded: 'Would it be becoming for a leader to flash his Rolex gold watch when times are bad? What would this signal?' I did not ask him about this gold pen. I did not need to. I felt foolish. What a man! Gentle, honest and empathetic, he set a great example of public behaviour. Between what he said and what he did, there was not a whisker's gap. The India visit came to an end, and the big man flew back. No gala dinners and unnecessary spends, no Mercedes Benz cars to move around the city. Just a modest Toyota sedan. I was lost in thought. It was great lesson for me. In difficult times, his actions spoke louder than his words.

6
Conviction Drives Culture

Many years ago, there was a sprightly young man, Prem Singh, a CHRO, who was working in one of those great organizations, a culturally vibrant place to work at. In those days, we did not have the 'Great Places to Work' list—if we had, this organization would certainly find a place on it, perhaps in the top ten. It was a small company, and while it neither boasted of a great revenue nor was it listed on the bourses, yet there was a certain attraction to this company. A certain aura. Its CEO, Pradeep, was a handsome man who led from the front. He empowered his people and loved to sit along with his leaders in the thick and thin of business. It attracted some very good talent, and I felt that much of it was owed to its CEO, a very fine man who was both genuine and charismatic. Prem, the CHRO, led a small team, and this mid-sized firm, with a large heart. It was a dream company to work for.

As part of his regular meetings, Prem met one of his senior members, who dropped a bombshell that he was going to quit the firm. No amount of speaking to him could hold him back. He held an important portfolio, and it was getting to be difficult to replace that position. It was a big blow to Prem, as this person was a key member of his leadership.

One day, a woman came to meet Prem. Nirmala, or Nimmy as she was usually called, had quit her job some years ago to raise her child. Her daughter was now fairly self-sufficient, and Nimmy had managed to get some house help. So, she was all set to return to the workplace. Prem was really happy to have met someone like her. She was a wonderful professional who came with great experience and from a very good business school. He was looking at Nirmala as a replacement for the person who had resigned.

However, in those days, if there was a gap in anyone's resumé, it was regarded as a major fault, even if it were a woman and it was understood that there could be breaks. It did not seem normal or wise to pick someone like her, for the break in her career was almost six years. Prem thought nothing of it and started the interview. He wanted to know the locus of her motivation and why she wanted to join his firm when she had lots of choices. She said that she wanted a smaller organization that would give her the latitude to exercise some choices of work and the way she would like to work. This part sounded a bit strange to Prem. He played along and kept his concerns to himself. Somehow, he felt she could make a difference.

Just when the conversation was progressing to the point of a job offer, Nirmala said that she wanted flexibility—work from home, work part-time and work at will, at least for a year or more, as she still had to look after her child. In those days, these flexibilities were unheard of. Prem heard himself agreeing to each of these requests. He said he would help her right through her year of raising her child and perhaps as long as she needed, till she felt comfortable coming in regularly to work. The candidate was very happy. She kept smiling.

The conversation on compensation did not seem difficult. She would have taken any compensation that Prem offered. But Prem was different. He looked up the value chart and the compensation range and made sure he paid her fairly. It was the least he could do for someone wanting to come back to work. There was no policy allowing such work style; in extending these unwritten benefits to her, he was breaking many policies. Nonetheless, he felt it was the right thing to do. However, he did not tell his boss at the time of the job offer to Nirmala. This was one of the biggest decisions of his life.

Later, he met his colleagues at the executive meeting and mentioned it to them, and they descended on him, reminding him that the 'policy' reigned supreme and that he had been high-handed. It was a long discussion, and convincing his colleagues was easy, for the culture was supportive. All this was in the early 2000s, when such things were unheard of. The woman joined the firm. Nimmy turned out to be one of the best members of his team, and she rose from strength to strength. She was a really a refreshing professional who brought in a zing to the place. She managed to put more into her job than anyone else. Her energy when she was at the workplace was infectious.

Prem, the HR head, moved on. He had long forgotten about what he had done in the organization when he was there. Nimmy did not. The only recollection I have of this story is when she was at a national event as a speaker. As always, she spoke passionately about her positive experience early on in her life. She spoke about how her manager had done something for her that was unthinkable at the time. He gave her flexibility. There were no laptops in those days and her manager trusted her with work—do the thinking part from home, and the doing a zing can be done at the workplace, as he said to her. Even as she was recounting her story, it left a deep impact on me as I was in the audience listening to her. Her manager broke all the rules for her. And over time, it became a policy. The ability to do things for others is within us, and it is for us to break the rules. People of influence can support people who need a helping hand at times. The manager could have flung the rule book at her and stood his ground, and it would have been correct. He chose to experiment with the rules, bend and break them. Flexibility starts with us being flexible in our mind.

Nimmy's story reminded me that it is not the policy that drives culture, but conviction about what is right that drives culture and thereby the policy—and happiness at work.

7

A Few Beautiful Gifts along the Way

There are things that one remembers long after they happened. Indelible memories. I was in middle school in one of the more famous schools of Chennai. It was special because it was one that started classes with prayers every day! The teachers were awesome; most of them, anyway. They were very demanding and made us do some impossible things. Even now, I remember the thrill of anticipation, waiting for the teacher to come in with new ideas and new knowledge; it fills me with nostalgia and makes me smile. The school gave us many gifts; they would always be surprises. I loved books, and once in a while, I would get books as prizes. Treasured for a long time, today they are lost and I am sure I would not find them in the hundreds that I have purchased and gathered along the way. The school had classes on art. All schools have them; what was special was that we were encouraged to give our art pieces as gifts to someone we admired. I did not get a single gift but gave what I made—with a lot of persuasion, because the receiver was not pleased with my art pieces. I was not good at art.

The teachers gave us time. That, I think, was the finest gift we received. They would spend endless hours with us. Some of us were not good at Math, but they would not be mad at us. They expected high standards from us. One or two students would fail their examinations, and the teachers were always there for the disappointed kids to console them. I have seen the worst of my classmates' fears about their success in life abate when they met the teachers. There were no parent–teacher meetings in those days. A lot of emphasis was placed on meeting with students. If you did well, they would still spend time with you, although it was much less than those who did not do well. Even those few minutes were precious. They had a lot of respect for students and I learnt this from them, the way they dealt with us in the highs and lows of our student life.

I remember many incidents from my school life. One thing stands out among the multitude of incidents I remember: the Ethics exam. The teacher, Ms Prema, was very clear that she wanted the whole class to be the best in her subject. She used to warn us about a 'surprise test'. We never believed her, for she had never sprung a test of this sort in a very long time. One day, out of the blue, she said that she was going to give a surprise quiz. I was completely unprepared. I was worried that I would fail the test. It would be ten questions and we were not to write long answers, she said. I started on the test paper with trepidation. Fortunately, it was not too difficult, but I was sure I did not get all the answers right. Not too bad for someone who had not prepared for it. I preferred to spend more time with the Math and Science subjects. Ethics was somewhere lower down in the pecking order of my studies.

Sundar stood first—not something one would expect. He was a backbencher and what you would call a middling pupil. Ms Prema was someone who gave a gift to anyone who aced one of her tests. Not all teachers did this. The teacher gave him a prize—a beautiful, shiny green pencil with an eraser at one end. I would have given my right arm to get such a prize. Sundar's name was called out. He stood up, head down. We thought that he would be the happiest boy in the class. Not Sundar. He did not speak. After some coaxing from Ms Prema, he looked up and mumbled something. She asked him to speak a little louder. Ms Prema could wait no longer and went up to him. She gently held his shoulder and asked him again. Sundar said that he had copied from a slip of paper and that he was not worthy of the gift. Ms Prema did not say anything. Normally, she would take off like a rocket at such instances. She asked Sundar to come to the front of the class. She then praised him for his honesty. She said it took guts to do what he had just done. She said this was ethics in action. The pencil was to be his. I never forgot that gift, for Sundar gave it to me at the school farewell. The pencil is with me, for it represents something that is precious—the courage to speak the truth.

The college that I went to was like the school I studied in. It started each Monday with prayers. Today I see that it instilled some culture in a boy who was overwhelmed by too many things flying at him. Vivekananda College was special. It made us spend time beyond studies in activities such as the National Cadet Corps and sports. The advantages of all-round development are obvious. I had taken up Mathematics. It was a subject that I was not keen on, but that is what I got as an area of specialization. We did not have too many choices back then. Sometimes, it is depressing if you do not do well.

In all this growing up, I remember Prof. Ramamurthy. He made Math seem so interesting. He used to look at the blackboard with affection and admire the formulae. To him, all of this was magical. In turn, we loved his lectures. His parting words, when I left the college, were: 'If you are from Vivekananda College, you will always do well in your life.' This got planted into my subconscious, I guess. Many times, when I am down and almost out, I remember these words of my professor. I should be doing well, after all, as I am from that college! At a subliminal level, it affected me positively. A wonderful gift.

My grandmother was another of those generous people. She gave me the gift of imagination. She said that all I needed to do was to 'think of something' and then work hard towards it. She said that many would join hands to make me win. She had not read Rhonda Byrne's *The Secret*. It was way before Rhonda's time. Several bosses gave me gifts—one gave me the gift of laughter, another showed me how to be a good 'boss', a third flew me out to New York to meet him at his favourite restaurant and in the course of the evening told me that 'I was a good man'. They all affected me deeply. They cared. I distinctly remember the boss who had a massive disagreement on my self-appraisal and said that I had underrated myself. He went on to upgrade my rating, saying it was only fair. What a gift!

I keep getting gifts each day—the company of friends, gentle words of encouragement and smiles that go a mile. I remember I have a responsibility—to pass it on and pay it forward. In this wonderful world of work and life, we have a duty to make someone's life a bit better. Even if it takes a bit of an effort. It's well worth it. We all have work to do besides receiving gifts: paying it forward.

8

A Lift, a Fall and Lessons Learnt

It was promotion time. A stressful time of the year for everyone. Managers had to propose the names of those they wished to promote, and there would be a meeting with a lot of other managers, and ultimately a list would be prepared for the management to approve. This consensus meeting would be rife with arguments for and against candidates that were proposed. Aspirations ran high within the group of people who thought that they could make it to the proposed promotion list. There were a limited number of positions available, and the list was getting bigger with every meeting. I was a new leader and it was a difficult job. There are prejudices and biases that are never articulated in plain English but find expression in different ways.

A small group of us were to decide on the final list of promotions, for we were the 'management'. It was a close call, and we could promote only a few. You reward for performance and promote for potential. This is so easy to understand, but how does it play out? Then there is the 'recency' effect to keep in mind. As I mentioned, I was not all that experienced as a leader. I also think that it was a good way to test me out in my new leadership role. I had enunciated the whole concept of performance and potential. At mid-managerial levels, you look beyond performance at potential. There were arguments for tenure in the role. There were people who had spent a lot of time in a role, but I was not sure if they deserved to be promoted.

There was a case that was a difficult one: Gaj, a manager who was to be promoted to a senior manager, was debated ad infinitum. Finally, we decided we would give Gaj a year more before we promoted him. Gaj was a great performer and a pillar of the recruitment function. I knew he would be hugely disappointed. He had been building up expectations around it and had spoken to his leader as well. But the decision was made. Gaj was almost there but needed some more time, we decided. We would stay with one more year of watchful guidance to prepare him to be a senior manager the coming year. It was left to his supervisor to speak to him. This conversation would be important, as it would set expectations of the why and the what of the promotion and how it could happen.

The reporting manager was supposed to speak to Gaj in the next couple of days to convey the news to him. His manager was diffidently unwilling and said that he was still not convinced we were right; the candidate deserved to be promoted. Now, leaders were taking positions for and against the promotion. Ultimately, I called the reporting manager and asked him to inform Gaj that he was to wait for a year.

This crucial conversation did not happen, as I discovered much later. Preparing him for the role of a senior manager was to be a journey in itself. It was not promotion, but more a preparation for promotion. This time round, he would be well-rewarded with a handsome bonus for the good work he had done. All tied up in a bow. Nice and easy.

I was on leave for a couple of days. I came in to work and checked to see if all was well. It was lunchtime and I went to the lift, and a small group of people entered. As did Gaj, the manager who had not been promoted. As soon as the lift started, Gaj confronted me and asked why he was not promoted. I kept my voice level and told him to meet me in my office. He was persistent, and I was getting annoyed. Gaj then raised his voice and, looking around him, made a provocative statement—that it was an unfair organization. At this point, I blurted, 'You need to have it in you to be promoted, and you don't have it in you, not yet. Be patient.' There was deathly silence. The lift stopped and the door slid open.

I knew I had made a mistake, a big mistake. I should never have spoken to him in the lift in front of other people. To make it worse, some of them were part of his team. He was visibly shaken. The others in the lift went their ways.

I immediately pulled him aside and apologized to him for saying what I had. He just stared at me. I tried to reason with him. I asked him if his reporting manager had spoken to him. It was obvious that he had not been spoken to. Gaj did not know what was in store for him, that we were preparing him for a senior role. He had been just left out in the cold, with no idea of what the company had in mind. He felt unappreciated and unrecognized. The way I had spoken to him crushed him completely.

A week later, he tendered his resignation. I knew I had made a mistake and tried to make amends. I spent hours trying to persuade him to stay. He refused. I had fallen in his eyes as a leader. Over the next month or two, I engaged him in several chats. I guess that by the time he left, he had forgiven me for my moment of intransigence. Today he is a well-known leader in a reputed organization. I still bump into him and pull him aside and take a moment to apologize to him. He is always gracious and laughs it off. I lost a wonderful man. I was looking for a perfect promotion: the perfect person in the role. A perfect person who never exists.

I learnt an important lesson in that lift that day. Managing my emotions is important, and understanding the emotions of others even more so. Another lesson I learnt: it is better to take a chance on a promising person, possibly not the perfect person, than to hold back. Pass over your rules, not a promotion. Today I live by the rule that it is better to chance it on someone who may be 70 per cent ready than to look for a perfect fit. In those days, I was not that wise. I'm still learning.

Habits and Behaviours

Depending on what they are, our habits will either make us or break us.
We become what we repeatedly do.

—Steven Covey

I believe in habits. Small habits that make big changes. How do we see this through small stories of mindfulness and take small steps that become powerful ways to engage with the self? What is goodness, completed work, doing small things exceedingly well and speaking up, in particular when most needed? Do they matter? Yes, indeed! They don't just take people ahead in work, they save lives! There are stories of apparent wastrels with catapults ending up as PhDs! Inspiring stories of passion and drive.

We often judge others—harshly. If we are in a position of power, it can be even more difficult not to do so. It is a human characteristic, I guess. And yet, over time, there have been so many examples of those who make a big difference to their lives by the simple act of keeping to what they are exceedingly good at. We learn a lot from those around us. Even the driver of a car can make a great impact on us. Several do, but we don't keep count of them. So, what do they do that inspires in us the one change that makes a big difference? The dazzle of brilliance? Perhaps not. Something done repeatedly so that it becomes second nature to us, like the steering wheel of a car which becomes an extension of ourselves as we drive along the road.

1
Mindful Timelessness

I met her in the airport lounge the other day. As ever, immaculate in her crisp light-coloured saree, with warmth in her eyes. She was on a call and, although she had a Kindle in her hand, she was not looking at it. She was the personification of concentration. I watched her for five minutes, which is a long period of time if you are looking to catch someone's attention. I dared not interrupt her, out of respect. Suddenly, she looked up, and the moment she saw me, she excused herself from the call in the most gentle of ways, rose and gave me an affectionate hug. I was so grateful to see her after a long time. We got talking. Speaking to her was like picking up from where we had left off a conversation minutes ago, though it had been many years. She had that magic. I could speak to her for hours, and I could listen to her for years. She was Dr Indira Parikh, professor of organizational behaviour at the Indian Institute of Management, Ahmedabad. A popular professor. There are many in the world who would consider her their mentor. I was in that long list of such people, way down in the list though.

Even as I was speaking to her, I kept an eye on the time, just to make sure I did not miss my flight. One can get lost in conversations with Dr Parikh. We had some twenty minutes to go before I would get an announcement for boarding. The intensity of the conversation was palpable. And the 'how' of such a conversation was not lost on me.

Some years ago, I had once asked Indira how she was able to make each minute work for her. She was a lead facilitator at the Indian Society for Individual and Social Development, an NGO which held many events and programmes on 'sensitivity', also known as 'human process work'. We had a lot of time together between the programmes with the facilitators.

More than once, I asked her about the 'magic' of how to make the moments count in any conversation. She would always smile and not respond to the question, and we would speak about something else. I came away from such chats even more intrigued about it. I was increasingly determined to get the answer and believed that she was not telling me the 'secret'.

One day, I accosted her with a pleading smile and begged her to tell me her secret, for it would make a difference to my life. As always, she smiled. She asked me to meet her in the evening. It was a great moment for me and I was thrilled. I felt that this meeting would be really special, and it was.

The spot we sat in was not really a quiet one. I did not care. I just wanted to listen to her. She told me that many years ago, when she was a young bride, she and her late husband, Dr Hemant Parikh, a scientist, were invited to attend a grand dinner ball in Stockholm, Sweden, on the tenth of December. The tenth of December? My eyes widened. 'Nobel Prize winner announcement?' I asked. She smiled and said yes, it was the Nobel Prize investiture ceremony. She mentioned that she was very young. She was very excited. She was not sure what she was to wear. All around her in the ballroom were men in the finest dark suits. She was the only one in the entire room who was in a sari, dark silk with a yellow border. The women invitees, perhaps the wives of Nobel laureates or themselves winners, were in evening gowns or black dresses. She suddenly found herself the cynosure of all eyes, the centre of attention. Many of the Nobel laureates of that evening went out of the way to meet her and spend a few moments with her. They were always followed by their entourage, their personal assistants. She was overwhelmed by all the fanfare around, she said to me. I was lost in her story. She said, 'In a moment of innocence and naivety, I asked one of the Nobel laureates if I could have an hour to talk with him in his office the following day to know more about him and his work.' There was a shocked silence, as no one would dare ask their precious time of such luminaries. The personal assistant was speechless.

The Noble winner didn't turn a hair. He was a kindly man and he agreed. His assistant quickly told Indira that she could meet the great man for fifteen minutes the following morning. She was asked to come in early so he was not kept waiting.

Indira arrived early next day. She was nervous as she walked into the stately building. The PA was waiting for her. At the appointed time, she was ushered into the Nobel laureate's presence. The big, airy room was flooded with natural light from big windows at the far end, before which stood a large mahogany desk. The gentleman, who was seated behind the desk, got up and met Indira halfway across the room. He was grace personified, said Indira. There was a great calmness about him. They spoke for a long time—a long, long time. Then, as gently as she had been ushered in, she was escorted out after a handshake. During their conversation, there had been no calls, no interruptions. Only the two of them, talking to each other. Indira smiled again. That long meeting, she said, had lasted all of fifteen minutes!

She had not told me this story earlier. Mindfulness, focus, and a deep sense of care and respect for another stretch time. It was incredible. I could feel the same thing whenever I was with Indira. Now I understood. Some things are worth learning and practising. Being in the moment: sans mobile, sans distraction, sans disruption. Concentration and focus on the individual and the conversation. That intensity, I guess, was what makes a Nobel laureate. I had never got round to asking her how she managed to do so much in such a short time.

This time, too, as we sat in the airport lounge, we were deep in conversation. My flight was announced, and my watch showed it had been all of eighteen minutes. Seemed like an hour. I am deeply in gratitude, Indira. For in your company, time is timeless.

2

Of Missed Flights and Goodness

Let me call him AB. He was a very senior person in the HR community. He ran his own firm. In meetings, he was always articulate and made his points clearly. I did not know AB very well. He was genial and friendly. And a bit inscrutable, I thought.

I had been invited to a meeting that AB was attending, too. I was unsure what to say, as the people in the room held such a variety of wildly divergent views. In all the cacophony in the room, I was getting bored and was not sure where this would all lead. Then I heard his voice ringing through the room, clear and soft. That day, I looked at his arguments in a biased way, no different from any other day. Such was my confidence about my 'instincts'. We broke for tea before the last few minutes of the meeting.

AB looked at me and headed in my direction. I was not sure what to say. He started a chat with me in his suave way, and I was wondering what he could possibly get from me. We had coffee and made small talk. This was the first time that I had had a private chat with him. He was good company. He smiled a lot and was easy to speak to. He could get me to be myself. Such was his 'skill'. After the meeting, he offered to drop me to the airport. I demurred, but he insisted and I agreed. Nice car, his BMW. He drove the car himself. He kept up a running conversation about interesting subjects. We reached the airport a good two hours before my flight. He parked his car and offered to have some coffee with me and keep me company. He was doing some 'business development', I thought. He had an hour to spare, he said.

The coffee arrived, and I was keen to get to the boarding gate and wait it out with a book for company. Out of the blue, a lean young man with a hint of worry on his forehead came up to our table. AB looked at him and asked him if all was well with him. The young man hesitatingly asked us if we could help him. He was going to Srinagar. He had missed his flight and the airline would not take him on the next without a fresh ticket, something they insisted he had to purchase and which was expensive. He had no money to buy the ticket. He had missed the flight as there was waterlogging in the area where he lived owing to an unexpected downpour, and he had barely managed to come to the airport.

He came to our table as we were the only suited gentlemen in the coffee shop, and he thought we could wield some influence. I was not sure what to do. AB did not hesitate. He simply asked some questions of the young man to make sure that he was a genuine passenger. The man, a Kashmiri, was lost and seemed helpless. AB told me that it was important to help the man in trouble and did not even wait for a response. I found myself running to the reservation counter, following AB. He met the reservation manager and spent the next thirty minutes speaking with a passion that I have never seen before in my career. He ended by saying that we ought to be gentler with our Kashmiri brother. Rulebooks were thrown at us by the reservation manager. AB would not give up. I added my two rupees' worth, supporting AB. Finally, the reservation manager relented and a fresh ticket was issued for a flight the next day—something that is seldom done. The only condition was that it was a non-refundable ticket. All thanks to AB, who went all out for a complete stranger who had approached us. I could not understand why anyone would do this, but I was happy it ended happily.

AB need never have done this. He could have just asked the man to find another person or even ignored him. Yet, he did neither. He stood up for someone he did not know from Adam, a complete stranger. AB also did not allow any big drama of gratitude. He made it look easy in the eyes of a stranger who had almost given up hope of getting back to his family in time. He simply smiled and gave him a hug. The young man was shedding tears of joy. He held his hands and thanked him. AB simply asked for another coffee for the young man and ordered a couple of doughnuts. He did not indulge him with money.

We walked out of the coffee shop. Time to leave, he said nonchalantly. He waved to me and started for his car, and I headed for the check-in desk. Then I stopped, turned, and rushed back to AB. I gave AB a big hug, holding on to him for a few moments. AB looked at me gently and smiled again, waved and walked away.

How easy it is to judge someone—sometimes unfairly! How easy it is to form an impression about someone and never worry about it. How easy it is to not even bother to validate the closely held views about someone! A simple act of kindness witnessed at close quarters left me in wonderment. Respect does not usually grow in an instant. In my case, it did. And I was acutely aware of my failing—my inability to see the goodness beyond the image I had held of the man. Perhaps it is the same as impaired vision. In my heart, I thanked the young man for opening my eyes. The time I spent with AB was precious. I had felt the extra warmth of kindness when I hugged Aquil Busrai.

It took a missed flight to understand the goodness in someone. It did.

3

Of 'Completed Staff Work'

A friend sent me his daughter's resumé. He wanted me to check if it would be suitable for my firm. I looked at the resumé. Richa had great academic credentials. She had graduated from good universities, and her introduction letter was very well-written. Normally, I ask someone to check out a resumé. This one, for some reason, got me hooked. I asked my assistant to schedule an interview. My assistant checked to see if I wanted to interview the girl personally, as she found it unusual.

At the appointed hour, Richa came into the conference room. She was very businesslike and had a pleasant demeanour. The interview went off well. She had worked for Teach For India, a non-government organization that had some wonderful teachers, all young minds who gave a lot of their time helping the underprivileged with their learning. When I asked her about it, she said that it was something that one 'had to do', for it was unfair for someone to be denied education. She had strong views on service to the community. I liked her, and although she had no formal background in human resources, I thought she was the kind of professional we needed in the firm.

An offer letter was sent to her, and we did not hear from her for quite some time. This was unusual. She was not responding to any calls. I was a tad upset and called my friend and told him about the employment offer to her. He said that I would hear from her, and soon. It seemed rather cryptic.

I found an email from her in my inbox; a longish mail. It was respectful and said that she would not be able to take up the offer, as she felt the only reason we hired her was that her father was my friend. There was undue influence, and so she had decided to decline the offer. I was amused and called up my friend. I said that now I was even more determined to get her into the firm, as I found her principled and value-driven. After a few calls to her—yes, she took the calls and then she joined in a week.

Richa is one of those professionals you really want on your team. She is blessed with a quality that makes her very special. We had assigned her to a very demanding manager. He was very picky, expected the best from his team and did not suffer mistakes lightly. One day, I chanced upon him and saw and then he was all smiles. I asked him why he was so happy. It was to do with Richa and her 'completed staff work' thing, he said. This was a term I did not understand and pressed for some explanation. Instead, he said he would allow for me to see it in action. 'Let me show you,' he said. He called Richa in my presence and asked her to get some data regarding attrition, something that would take a couple of days to prepare, as we all know.

Later that evening, he called me to his office. The data was neatly collated, and there was a separate annexure that had a lot of insights from the attrition data. It also had some suggestions about what could be done for a few individuals who were at risk of leaving the firm. I was really impressed and wanted to meet her. Her manager obliged. Richa was bright and full of energy. I quizzed her about 'completed staff work', a term that I was intrigued by.

She said she had learnt it from the first manager in her career, an army officer and a veteran. When a task is completed on time, accompanied by useful details—something that is not asked for—including choices and recommendations, it is 'completed staff work' or CSW, she said proudly. It worked best when there were decisions to be made and insights would certainly help. I asked her for some insights from the report and even asked her to predict attrition, and she was ready with that. She had even put up a work paper on 'how to anticipate attrition, and work to addressing it'. She also told us that there was a department where there would be attrition and it was owing to a certain manager. She had done some work with members of the team. She added that she hoped it would be kept confidential. I just smiled at the sensibilities that Richa held for her job.

The key to CSW was to anticipate what a manager would need, add your insights and offer choices. It needs a bit of understanding of the circumstances and context, Richa added. You also needed a supportive manager. It was my turn to smile. I understood why her manager was so cheerful. I had learnt something from Richa, and I thanked her. Her manager told me he had instituted CSW in his entire team and asked Richa to teach its principles to them. It almost seemed like a movement.

I asked Richa how she managed all of this. She was a bit embarrassed and said that perhaps her on-the-job training at Teach For India helped her. They had to do more than just teach at the institution. They had to think ahead and prepare for classes not just for the coming day, but for the week and the year. Teach For India's loss was our gain. I was beaming and picked up the phone and called up my friend, Richa's father, and thanked him.

As I moved towards the close of the year, I made a promise to myself—I would put to work what I had learnt about completed staff work—a promise I was determined to keep that year and beyond.

4

A Bumpy Road, a Smooth Ride

As I have mentioned before, I started my career as a management trainee with a well-known multinational. It was at a factory manufacturing explosives for the mining industry in what is now Jharkhand, a state rich in minerals. This was almost thirty years back, and the roads were not what we see today. The nearest government district headquarters were some sixty kilometres away. I was told that management trainees were usually sent to such places to follow up on matters in the labour department that needed a gentle nudge. It was not a great posting, and it was my turn to do what I thought of as a 'silly' job. I could not understand why they needed someone from one of the finest business schools to do it. As you can see, I had a large chip on my shoulder.

One day, my manager called and asked me to go to Giridih district to follow up on a file on labour. I protested, but he would not hear of it and told me that a car would arrive at seven in the morning the following day. He phoned the administration team and told them to send driver Ram Lal Singh, no one else. My friends told me that it was a two-hour ride from our factory in Gomia, to the town of Giridih.

The following day, I was getting ready to leave and seething at the thought of the 'silly' job that I had been asked to perform. I came down from the first-floor apartment where I stayed and headed to the car that was to take me to town. It was then that I noticed something strange.

The driver, Ram Lal, with a soft velvety cloth in hand, was burnishing the black Ambassador car to a fine shine. I had expected a driver who would be sitting in the car, waiting for his passenger. I walked up to him and asked him what he was up to. Ram Lal said that he was polishing his car with wax. I remarked that I had heard the roads were nothing great and the dust would ruin the shine anyway, so it was pointless. He said, 'Sir, I love my car and I love my job. There is no work that is small, and while the dust may yet settle back, if I did not polish the car, it would look shabby and reflect poorly on me and the company I work for.' Ram Lal was no ordinary driver. He was wearing a spotless starched white uniform, looking very prim and proper. Even his shoes were shined to a mirror finish.

I got into the car and was about to slam the door shut when suddenly Ram Lal was there. He gently closed the car with a click. 'I did not want the door slammed shut,' he said. He started the car and shifted gears in a gentle sort of way.

He talked to me during the drive; he said work was divine and he was fortunate to be working. I could see that he was passionate about his job. He spotted potholes in the distance and navigated them with elan; even apologized it was a bad bump. I reached Giridih in all of ninety minutes, and it was one of the best of rides despite the bad roads. I complimented him on that. He was beaming with pride. He said that a car should be driven as if there were a baby in the back seat, with due care and deference to the life he was responsible for. He had won me over, right there. What passion!

I walked into the labour office. I met the officer with a smile on my face. I put my all into the few minutes that I had with the officer, and he appeared to be happy with me. The job was done. I was happy. I was now confident that I had got the 'silly job' done to perfection. I thanked the officer and returned to the car and to Ram Lal. He was polishing up his car. It was nothing new to me now: the dust had been wiped clean, and his car gleamed. We drove back and I was absorbed in an even more engaging conversation with him. He talked about the value of respecting work and doing it with devotion. He told me that he had learnt all this from his 'babuji'—his father. He said whatever job one had to do, it had to be done right and with love. Another thing he learnt was that when one was working, there was no place for a 'no' in it. His own way of saying that he would do all that was expected of him.

Ram Lal had not gone to school and just about knew how to read the road signs. His best friends were the garage mechanics. He said that we must know our friends at work—those whose help we might need at any time; they should be ready to help and deem it a privilege to serve you. Seriously? Yes, he said. He said that everyone needed some appreciation and so, he always made sure to meet the mechanics and give them positive feedback about the car and how she was in fine fettle, and thank them. They should puff up with pride in their work. It was the same with all of us. He had picked up some sweets for them from Giridih town, he added. We arrived back in Gomia, and I thanked him for his education.

The following day was Teachers' Day. I thought of Ram Lal, my greatest teacher, and went to thank him for driving the greatest lesson of work into me, and that it happened so early in my career. The chip on my shoulder was much smaller post that trip. It was then that I remembered my manager, who had insisted that Ram Lal be my driver. It was part of my induction to excellence. I still remember Ram Lal each year on Teachers' Day. What a drive!

5

Speak Up When Most Needed

It was one of those late-night conference calls, with the top leaders of the company on it. You name it—the CEO, CFO, CHRO, business leaders—the who's who of the company, right from the top of the leadership ladder downwards, were all there. A delicate matter had to be discussed.

It was like this. Some months ago, an engineer left the shores of India for Canada on a project. It was a traditional project, something that he was an expert at. Next, he was moved to the US office, as they too needed such an expert. In a short time, he had impressed his leaders with his work. Unfortunately, he fell ill and was taken to a hospital where they diagnosed his ailment as the dreaded encephalitis—brain fever, potentially fatal. He was in the hospital for over five months, and there was no improvement in him. The doctors gave up and recommended he be moved to a hospice—a euphemism for allowing to meet his Maker in the quiet confines of a room that was outside of the hospital rigmarole. Big bills at the hospital and attendant medicines had not helped. He had run out of insurance and the company was helping out. His wife back home in India was anxious, as were his friends and family. What should be done next?

This call was an important one. It was scheduled for all of sixty minutes. The leaders were to be apprised of the situation and the decision to be taken was a delicate one. The call started. Someone said that the case was a hopeless one—the lad should be put out of his misery—and advocated the hospice route. Another said that a better hospital was needed. Yet another mentioned that the man's wife in India was insisting on his being moved to India as that would be most appropriate. Shifting a person in ICU would mean an air ambulance with ICU facility, and that meant a special aircraft would be needed. There were huge costs involved. Also, an air ambulance had to land at some airport enroute every five hours as per international rules, added another. It would cost a fortune to get him on a plane and send him to India.

There was a lot of debate on the relative merits of shifting the patient to India or keeping him in a hospice in the US and inviting his wife and family to the US to be with him till he passed away. The call veered towards the opinion that the exorbitant cost and the low chance of survival played in favour of a hospice option. The call was coming to an end, the decision almost taken. It was just another five minutes to go before a decision would be made and the call ended.

Also on the call was a shy junior manager who was overwhelmed with the presence of the high-ranking leaders on it. He had a view about how this matter was to be dealt. He was unsure though, there were too many bigwigs and he was overwhelmed. Dare he even say his piece? He had been quiet all along, his inner voice egged him on. With two minutes to spare, he hesitatingly started: 'Ladies and gentlemen leaders on the call, this boy would be alive had he not left the shores of India. He would be with his wife and family, and hale and hearty. He left the shores of the country as he was called to duty by his superiors. Like a good soldier, he went where he was told to go. He served the firm the best he could. We have a responsibility towards him. India deals with more such cases of brain fever than other countries, and there is an outside possibility that he could be cured by the doctors here. Let us give moving him to India by an air ambulance a chance. Perhaps it could work. It is my sincere request—the soldier did his part when he was called for duty, and now it is our turn, we have a duty too: let us bring the soldier home.' He was sweating, but he had said his piece. There was a long silence. After what seemed like an eternity, the CEO spoke up: 'Folks, I agree. If he had continued his work in India, perhaps he would not be in this condition with brain fever. We carry a precious responsibility, and we have always put people first. The lad has served us well in the battle. Let us send the soldier home.'

Fast forward. An air ambulance was organized. A colleague of the patient was allowed to travel with him. Then started the endless paperwork that would assist in the air passage sans any impediments at the airports along the way. After all the landings and takeoffs at various airports enroute, the air ambulance finally landed in India. His wife was at the airport, as were a few friends. They rushed him to a top hospital that had been apprised of such a patient being enroute to their specialized care.

It was six long months of hospitalization, with a devoted wife in attendance. His friends would visit him, but all they could see was someone in near-coma and his wife, whose eyes expressed gratitude. Every now and then, she would ask the doctors if he would pull through. The doctors were most patient, and they always mentioned that the organs were in fine condition and that he would recover. His colleagues never gave up on him. They would visit the hospital more than they visited shrines. They would be discouraged by their friends, but for some reason, they never gave up.

One day, at last, Amit went back to work, to thunderous applause from his colleagues.

The manager who had spoke up that day sported a smile. He had learnt his own lesson, as had many on the call—speak up when it is needed the most. It could save a life!

6
Falling in Line

I was leaving for Mumbai that morning. I normally travelled the evening before as it gave me the whole of the following day and I could start work early. I had to get up early and although I am an early bird, this was not my idea of what an early bird did. I felt more like a midnight owl. I woke up at 3 a.m. to catch a flight at half past six. My bags were all packed and the cab would arrive in time. All I had to do was shower and leave. My kids were fast asleep, and I planted a kiss on each of them. They were possibly half-awake and smiled. It is difficult to travel to another city, leaving behind children and a wife who is ever supportive of what you are doing. I hoped my dog would not bark; luckily, he was at his quietest. He just came by and wagged his tail. It would not take more than half an hour to the airport. We hit the expressway and there seemed to be traffic all over the place. I was wondering what had happened, even as the cab driver parked the car and pulled out my luggage.

It was one of those crazy Monday mornings at the airport. It was just after the holiday season and seemed to be the first day of work for everyone. Almost the entire city had converged to take a flight that day, it seemed. I saw long queues; I am sure you have shared that fear of missing a flight. I am used to getting way ahead of everyone to make sure that I do not miss a flight. On that day, it appeared that I should have landed the day before to be ahead in the queue. This was for the check-ins, where you collected your printed ticket. Yes, you had those things in those days, not so long ago. No fancy ticket-dispensing kiosks that one sees about these days. It was a long, serpentine line. Someone had helpfully set up the swim-lane-type tapes to regulate traffic. I was anxious and kept looking at my watch. The only person that I had for company was another passenger who had to catch the same flight, and he seemed nonchalant. Perhaps he did not suffer the anxieties that I did. Finally, I got my ticket, and it was another long queue past the security and then a sea of humanity waiting to get their luggage past the few X-ray machines and security people, who were clearly not used to seeing such a surge of people.

It was not an automated luggage system as you find these days in leading airports. First you had to get your hands on a couple of trays, which you would get with some difficulty. Thereafter, you had to stand in a queue with one hand carrying the trays and the other your possessions. You would then deposit the laptop, your jacket, mobile, etc., in one tray, and the other tray would take your shoes and any other odds and ends that you had forgotten. The stroller bag could go straight on to the carousel. That day, getting two of the prized trays was like getting a lottery ticket. A big fat one. Someday, I think, someone is going to make some great suggestion about how we should have a seamless way to deposit our luggage for airport scrutiny, which would be from the kerbside where the cab drops you off.

I was in one of those long queues that got you to secure your trays, and then you got into another queue to deposit your luggage. I almost made it to the tray lot when a big, well-muscled man walked in front of me and took a tray. Clearly, he had jumped the queue. I was touched to the quick but did not want to raise my voice and make any kind of protest. He seemed mean and in a hurry. He did not apologize or even mention that he had an 'earlier flight to catch', something that I would have happily allowed to pass. Except, that day, my inner voice did not shut up. I heard myself speak in a firm and polite way: 'Excuse me, sir. There is a queue here. Would you mind joining it, please? We have been standing in queues for long.' I looked at him and gave him a smile. My fellow queue guys looked at me in horror. None of them had spoken up. The hulk looked at me for a moment. Then he capitulated and meekly said, 'Oh, I did not know that.' A lie that I gladly glossed over and proceeded with collecting my two trays. He chose not to make eye contact. I murmured a 'thank you'.

Of course, next you join the queue for depositing the luggage, which I did, and then there was the physical check. That took a while, and I reached the other side to wait for my bags to get through the scanner. This was going to take time. I was happy that I had finally made it on the other side and all I needed was to get to the aircraft-boarding queue! Even as I was waiting, I espied the queue on the other side and saw the hulk waiting near the trays. Just then, another man sneaked in and took a tray and stood ahead of the hulk. This was interesting. The hulk politely said to him, 'Excuse me sir, there is a queue here, do you mind?' The man said, 'Oh, sorry. I did not know that.'

It seemed that the heavens smiled, as did I, for this whole business of 'falling in line' was falling in line! Just sometimes, you have to speak up and stand up for what you believe in, even in the face of consequences. It seems that others are watching you, and what goes around comes around!

7

Of Catapults, Passion and Success

I quite like catapults. They remind me of my childhood and the memories associated with a dear old friend of mine. This was in Nagpur, a lazy city then, in the heart of India. My friend in the all-boys high school was an interesting chap, Brian. Over time, he became my best friend. Brian's mother used to tell him that he ought to spend more time with the cleverest boys, because she thought that keeping the company of studious children would benefit her son. Brian was a colourful boy. He had varied interests. He went to church every Sunday. He was pious to a fault—and the added attraction was to see all the pretty girls there. He was lean and handsome and had a wide smile most of the time. He was easy to speak to, and we all liked him. I was envious of Brian.

Once, he planned to make catapults and sell them to friends. I knew the difficulty in selling such devices those days, since nobody really wanted to buy them. Brian insisted on making a catapult. Why this urge to make catapults? That was an interesting story. We had gone to an open field that had a tree loaded with berries. A catapult would come of use. We purchased one for ten rupees, a fortune in those days. It was a simple one. Made of a Y-shaped piece of wood with bands of rubber meeting in a leather dispenser in the centre. When he tried to use it, the wood snapped, and we were really upset. That is when he decided that he would make a catapult. I tried to dissuade him, but he was adamant.

He searched and gathered a few thin iron rods from a local scrapyard. After some hard work, he got them cut into the right shape and size. I was all but a bystander in all these escapades. He then got the V-shaped rods trimmed suitably in a nearby workshop so they would fit the palm of one's hand. It still was not suitable and did not look appealing, he said. He then dragged me to another place where he got ten of these V-shaped rods chrome-plated to make them look cool and shiny.

Now for the rubber bands. Brian took me to a railway scrapyard, an open field of junk discarded by the railways workshop. They had reams of discarded rubber beading, the kind that is used to line the windows in local trains. I found myself walking with him to another part of the city to a cobbler, who cut the rubber bands and stitched a piece of leather to the ends of two bands. He then tied the other ends of the bands to the ends of the V-shaped steel rod. Brian made sure that the centre piece of the leather was in the exact centre, with the rubber bands on each side equally adjusted for perfect alignment. He did this for each catapult and when he was satisfied, he thanked the cobbler and paid him his money, all of two rupees per catapult. When it was done, the catapults were works of art, shiny and functional. Yes, you would want to own one.

Brian had been working like a man possessed. Finally, he was ready with slick-looking catapults, all shiny objects of desire that everyone wanted to buy at a princely twenty-five rupees each. Now that is a huge price for a device that was deemed quite unimportant in those days! Each of the catapults was a masterpiece. You could see that Brian was happy. I admired him. He may not have been on top of the class in studies, but there was something about him. He was serious about anything that he did. I remember once he stood in a queue for several hours to purchase a Beatles album. The catapult money must have helped him buy that, I am sure. Another time, he decided he would build a radio and started from scratch. He was good at hockey. He dressed well. I would hang around with him a lot. There was so much to learn from him. I was good academically, but he was streets ahead in the ways of the world.

Months passed by, and my friend and I parted ways as he went on to live in Ahmedabad and I lost touch with him. Several years later, I just happened to visit Ahmedabad. I remembered that he stayed there. I found his address and was thrilled that I would get to meet my good old friend. I went to his house and met his mother. She was overjoyed. She told me that my friend lived in the US and that he had migrated there some years ago. She said he was a successful imaging scientist in the country. I couldn't believe my ears when she told me that he had studied physics. Surely not Brian! I would never have guessed it. She said that he had moved to the US and secured a PhD from the University of Michigan. Incredible! What a march forward!

It got me thinking. So, what was special about this guy, who was never big into studies? It was this—anything he did, he did with a lot of passion. If he had to buy a Beatles record, he would stand in long queues for hours to buy it (remember, in those days we did not have iTunes). If he decided to make a radio, he would not rest till he had made one. If he had to make a catapult, it would be the best one and anyone would be proud to own it. He invested passion in anything that he took up. He never let go till he finished his work. That was Brian.

Now, back to the catapult. It remains an iconic device in my life. It represents the passion of a beautiful mind that catapulted him to greatness. By the way, I managed to track him down in the US. Work took me there and one weekend, I travelled to San Francisco to meet him. We had a nice meal in the evening, chatted about life and laughed together. We remembered the good times of catapults and more.

Take a bow, Dr Brian Rodricks; you taught me something, and I owe you big.

Coaching

A good coach can change a game.
A great coach can change a life.

—John Wooden

No person is perfect. We all need help. How do we seek a coach, and what do we look for in ourselves? Conversations about coaching are engaging, for they are stories about how one became an athlete, others are about discovering the meaning behind the conversations, discovering the pupils' motivation, the coach's own commitment and more. Ultimately, it is about building one's confidence. Many coaches influence our lives in gentle ways; they leave indelible impressions on us.

Many a time, we have the potential in us and yet falter at the altar, the starting block. It takes a lot for anyone to move ahead, and sometimes a gentle nudge, or perhaps a forceful push, does the trick. Over time, we become coaches, having learnt that it is about time that we either discover something in us that would get us to succeed or find it in others and help them to succeed. In all such cases, it is about a mind-altering moment, the moment when we feel it is all-important for us to move ahead. That tipping point.

1
Mentoring and Why I Polish My Shoes

We all know that a compass is an instrument that provides direction. Some of the more sophisticated compasses have more to display than the usual directions. In any case, they are most useful in helping us find a certain orientation. An anchor provides stability to a ship and saves it from swinging wildly and foundering. A mentor helps us orient ourselves, find direction and points to our goals; a mentor provides stability and confidence in our journey, professional or personal, and helps us stay rooted to our goals. A mentor is the anchor and the compass in our lives that we need to get our ship to the shores of our choice.

In my career of several years, mentors have played an important role. I have been a protégé and, in more recent times, a mentor. Mentoring is a personal way of sharing knowledge and ideas and combining perspectives in new, motivating ways with your team members and peers. It is a developmental partnership—one that got me to do the most basic of work: polishing my shoes!

Over the years, I have been lucky to have had numerous colleagues and seniors as mentors. I still turn to many of them for advice and guidance. One of my first experiences of mentors in my professional life was my first boss, someone I can never forget.

I had been selected as a management trainee at a large multinational. I was doing the rounds of various departments and learning the business. I was moved to administration. The manager was a retired army officer. He had been on a short service commission. He was a genial man, very friendly; someone who you could approach at any time, day or night. His parties were legendary: evenings filled with plenty of bubbly and lots of cheer and laughter all around. At the same time, he was demanding of himself and others. He was prompt and worked hard. As young professionals new to work and to the workplace, we found he had a great impact on many of us.

There was something special about my manager. He had this knack of noticing the good in people more than their faults. He would also say so, that too in public. There were meetings where he would call out those had done good work.

I had a small team working with me. I had always been one who did not lose a moment to point out a fault in others. Many a time, I would put down others in front of my manager. It was my way of letting the person know who the boss was. Of course, my boss noticed this in me and could have easily pointed it out to me and given me some advice about it, but he didn't.

I never cleaned my shoes. I felt it was unnecessary and put it off for another day. Almost every day, my shoes were unpolished and muddied from walking on the road I took to work. I am sure he must have noticed it, as he was an army officer once, but he never said anything about this to me. A few months later, the season had changed: the rains were upon us. I was walking to work when suddenly, the sky opened up and it poured. I was fortunate I had an umbrella. But that did not protect my shoes. I had a meeting with my manager and was sure I would be late. I quickly cleaned myself up in the washroom and rushed to my manager's cabin. I reached his office, and he looked at me and said, 'Nathan, your shoes are polished, well done!' How was I to tell him that I had done nothing; the rains had removed the dust and perhaps the mud as well. I was feeling sheepish. I knew that he knew it had rained, but he chose to point out that the shoes were clean. It was gracefully said, with no tinge of sarcasm. I am positive that he had noticed the earlier times when they weren't clean, far less shiny. I thanked him, mumbled some inanities and walked away from his office.

The next day onwards, what do you think was the one thing I did before I set out to work? Yes, I was busy polishing my shoes! He caught me off guard, but at a time when something about me was right, as opposed to pointing out something wrong; something that I had been repeatedly doing wrong. It had a deep impact on me. This has been a memorable lesson, one that got me to notice people doing something right and to point it out. I realized early in my career, positive affirmations expressed to another are more powerful than negative comments and help change behaviour. This is a mantra that has been extremely helpful in my relationships as a professional.

Catching someone doing something right and paying them a compliment in a graceful way can be deeply energizing, both for the receiver and the giver. Even in small matters, it can have a deep impact. I have tried this with my mother, who, when I told her that she was looking beautiful in her new saree, said to me, 'So, what do you want?' and seemed to ignore my protestations. A few minutes later, though, she was preening herself in front of the mirror and clearly telling herself that she had a smart and sensitive son. Adding a dose of sincerity had magical powers.

Back to mentors. You can have a mentor for different aspects of your life. You can have a mentor for helping you with your finance, or a spiritual mentor, a technology mentor or a mentor for your career. Choose your mentor well: someone whom you look up to and who has the time and the patience to help you. Someone you can rely on to keep you honest when you falter. And, when you see someone who meets your standards, all you need to do is to reach out and ask that person. Over time, I have felt the need to choose new mentors, and that is equally important. So go on, find a mentor if you don't have one already, and work towards building a meaningful and successful association. Someone who can help you add value to yourself. Help you shine your shoes, shine your life. One thing more, I shine my shoes each day before I head to work. Thank you, Capt. Arvind Nautiyal.

2

The Source of Motivation

Kumar was sitting all alone. It was one of those days when he sat in the library staring blankly into a book that he neither understood nor cared to. A two-year programme at a premier institute is an essay in hard work and application of the mind in subjects that one could never relate to. Yet, the wise men and women who designed the course of education deemed it necessary to pound the students with archaic subjects and suggested that they commit to memorizing things that one could find in any book. He was just tired. He had worked hard to stay ahead in his class. He was not at the top of the class, but close enough—in the top ten. Getting into the portal of knowledge itself was an achievement, he rationalized. He kept tapping the table, looking at a thick book of nothingness. The librarian, a kind lady, walked up to him and asked if all was well with him. He nodded in the affirmative. What else could he do? It was her nice way of asking him to stop tapping the table!

He looked back at the past year. The summer programme would be up on them in a month. He had to find something that would be of use to himself and the company he would be joining for the summer internship. It was in this context he was looking at the book, lost in his dreams of a tomorrow that no one has ever seen. Just then, a friend of his, Vinay, walked past him, stopped and came back to his table. He looked at him and asked what he was doing. Stranger questions had been thrown at him. What would one do in a library? Read, of course. Refer perhaps and search for the right book. He looked back at Vinay and told him that he was reading something in the library. Vinay laughed. His voice was laden with sarcasm. He asked Kumar what he was going to read about and said that reading was pointless. Vinay added in a provocative voice, 'Kumar, you can do nothing. Even if you did your best, you can never be a topper in class.'

Kumar was very upset with this statement. He rose to his full height of five feet and six inches, looked Vinay in the eye and retorted, 'I can tell you this, Vinay, I will stand first in class for every single subject hereon. If there is one A+ grade, it will be mine. Just you watch, Vinay. Just you watch.' Vinay laughed it off and walked away, a dismissive hand waving in Kumar's direction. He was mocking Kumar. It was a bit too much for Kumar to take. He shouted at Vinay to see the final scores in the next exams.

Kumar then sat down, his forehead perspiring profusely. He had said something that he was quite unsure about. How could he make up the gap to get from the tenth position to the top of the class? He would give his best, for sure. He was upset that he had been provoked into making this rash statement, and to add to his discomfiture, there were a lot of people in the library.

The next few months and all of the year went in some serious studying. Kumar was determined to give his best to every subject, whether he liked it or not. He worked like there was not tomorrow. Weekends were a grind, making sure he could recount all that he had learnt. Time flew, and it was already time for the first semester exams. He not only passed with flying colours but was the topper of every exam that semester. Suddenly, he became a celebrity. His friends flocked around him and promised that he would get a top rank for sure. Kumar was more bothered that he should stand first in each and every subject in the exams. And he did it.

His summer internship was so good that the head of HR of the company where he worked gave him an A+. More accolades, awards and rewards followed. By the end of the second semester, it was well known that Kumar was fast catching up with the others who were at the top of the heap. Kumar would just not give up. He started teaching others as well. The third semester was upon them and the big question was not whether Kumar would ace the semester exams, but by what margin! The fourth semester was a light one, as it coincided with the placement season. Kumar stood first. In all, his cumulative grade point index had shot up to a number ahead, and he secured the top position in class. He was happy. He would show Vinay what he was made of!

On the way to the cafeteria, he met a professor who was known to be one of the finest at the institute; he was a kind man, too. He saw Kumar and asked him where he was going. Kumar blurted out that he had made it to the top of the class and wanted to share the news with Vinay. The professor asked Kumar if he could spare him a few minutes before the meeting with Vinay. 'Of course,' said Kumar. The professor asked him how he had made it to the top of the class when he had not even been in the top five. Kumar then recounted the incident with Vinay, who was the sole reason why he was at the top of the class, he said proudly. The professor looked at Kumar kindly and said, 'So, your motivation came in from an axis of provocation.' Kumar was puzzled. He asked the professor to explain it to him. 'Vinay challenged you, and you proved him wrong. This form of motivation is acting from an axis of provocation,' said the professor.

He then asked Kumar, 'Will you always have to search for another Vinay in your life for you to win the next big challenge? Why don't you consider working from within, from your own axis of 'evocation' instead?' Kumar looked at him in wonder. 'That way, you are your own master,' the professor added thoughtfully. Kumar was stunned. Yes, he was right. I am working from an axis of provocation, not evocation, thought Kumar. The professor gently patted Kumar's shoulder and walked away. Kumar did not move. He was lost in thought. Could he find his 'mojo' from within instead of from outside? He had just had the greatest coaching in his life. The need to make meaning from within; to set goals that are one's own and to work from within, of our choice instead of being provoked to act. This was deep and profound.

The meeting with Vinay did not matter at all. He turned around and headed to meet the librarian to thank her for her support. That meant a lot more to him. The search for his 'evocation' would begin.

3

When a Bargain Isn't One

My father taught me to shop for vegetables. His conversations were perhaps not so much about shopping as lessons along the way. Each Saturday morning, we used to set out to the bazaar at six o'clock. Fresh vegetables would have arrived, all nicely cleaned. He did not like to go to the supermarkets, as he thought that he would feel a sense of satisfaction if the money for the produce went straight to the farmers and their ilk. The vegetable bazaar was a place worth a visit. It was a sea of green. Vegetables were neatly laid out in piles on the ground upon jute sacking. Some parts of the bazaar sold certain vegetables, other areas had certain other kinds of vegetables. The leafy vegetables would always be towards the exit of the bazaar. Dad used to tell me that it was so arranged that one could purchase them on their way out and place them on top of the other vegetables, so the greens don't get crushed by the heavy ones like potatoes and beet.

Expectant vendors were waiting for the first visitor to their stalls. Anticipation was high. I walked with my dad, a stocky, genial man with a cherubic face. He took me all around the place and wished all the vendors a cheery morning while evaluating where the vegetables were freshest. He would also carefully note the price of each of the produce. Out of earshot of the vendor, he told me the prices of a certain vegetable at different stalls. He asked me to note them down in my head, and I had to let him know where to shop for the lowest cost. He also searched for some rare vegetables which were not normally available elsewhere.

Once in a while, he would stop at a pile of okra (lady's finger in India), bend down, pick up one and test its tenderness. He also taught me how to check all sorts of vegetables for freshness and tenderness. Finally, when he was done checking, he would tell me that we were ready. I would reel off the places where we would get the best deals. He would listen to me carefully. In the beginning, I never understood his ways. He would stop by some young vendors and engage them in long negotiations, settling with them for a price that was, according to him, the best. That apart, he would also choose some old vendor to buy vegetables from—vendors withered with age and wrinkles of days spent in the sun. Their price was always a tad more than others'. He would not bargain as hard with them. He would give in to their final number, although we could have picked up the same veggies from another place at a much lower cost. He said it was a sign of respect to the vendor. He did not care if we paid more—he said that they worked harder than us. Most of the older vendors would cry out to my dad to visit them. It was a game of sorts where they felt that they always won. He did not see it as losing. I learnt much from him: that it is important to know the lay of the land, be generous and kind, settle only for the best, even if it costs a bit more. Most of all, help someone who could do with your assistance.

Once it happened that we were negotiating with the unions. It was a long and hard-fought 'battle'. I had decided to take everything off the table and had pinned the unions to the ground with some pointed negotiations. They had no choice but to take the offer that I made to them. The union leader, Srinivas, was a wily leader; a good-natured man, too. He was past his prime, but he held sway over his followers. After the penultimate negotiation meeting, he called for a separate meeting with me. I was not sure if I should meet him, though I felt he was someone I could trust. I met him on common ground—in a conference room. I was way younger than Srinivas. He asked me a question: 'Sir, would you want a settlement that was in favour of the management, or one in favour of the union, or one that was fair to both?' What a question! I told him that I would choose the last option.

He smiled and said that the negotiations were such that they did not respect the unions. He asked me if I respected him. I was floored. I said I did and explained my predicament—we were worried about runaway costs. He said that the unions and the workmen would not want anything that jeopardized the factory and its running. He then offered to put off the final round until he was sure his workmen were happy with the proceedings. He said that a settlement must stand the test of time. I had heard these lines from my father. A settlement is a good one when each party feels that they have won the argument. My dad also said that it would be important to leave a little bit on the table. A sign of dignity and trust, he said.

The settlement that Srinivas signed with the management was one of the best for everyone all around. What was established was trust—something priceless.

These days, I try to visit the farmers' market at Mehdipatnam and take my sons too. Even today, in fond remembrance of my dad, I ask myself—what would he want me to do?

4

Security Checks and the Gift

This was some years ago. It was the time of the downturn. Tough times. I was not in the best of moods. I had a difficult task ahead of me. How do we make sure that we have no layoffs? And pay our people on time? The cash in the bank was rapidly depleting. I had no one to turn to. The Chief Financial Officer was calling me to ask me if I had some plans for the people. My CEO was a tough man, and he would not hesitate to make a tough call in any negotiation or on any normal day. This was different; it was dealing with the lives of people. He had asked for me, and this meant that he was searching for ideas. I had just stopped at the office security. The security guard, Jha ji, waved me forward but not till he had thoroughly checked my bag. He was the most respectful of the security guards at work. He would give a friendly smile to the employees, who had to suffer him opening their bags to check for anything forbidden in the workplace—guns or knives, for instance. Of course, he did not expect to find anything and gently zipped up the bags. Many times, I have noticed the wry looks of the employees, almost to say, 'Hey, you have seen me so very many times. Do you seriously think I have something to conceal? Do I look like a terrorist?'

I know of some who have even shouted at him for delaying them on their way to work. He would always be respectful and apologize for the inconvenience caused. The smile never died out. I could learn a thing or two from him. What a man! He made quite an impression on his colleagues and so, many of them would mimic his pleasant service. I often felt sorry for him and wondered what it meant for him to work this way each day, every day: no respite and having to make sure that no bag went unchecked. He was ever so respectful to one and all. Many of us smiled back at him with respect in our eyes. Perhaps he could sense what we were thinking.

My meeting with my CEO was a long one. We had to make some tough decisions. We had a few choices and, certainly, layoffs were one of them. There were arguments for and against the layoffs. We were known to be a caring firm. We had taken all the steps towards cost cutting; almost shaved the cost to the bone, as it were. Not enough, said the CEO. I proposed that those in leadership take a 20 per cent cut in our salaries. This way, we could save the jobs of our people. It would mean that we had to communicate to 'our people', the management, as well. The plan was a good one; it seemed honest. We also decided to put off any salary hikes in view of the downturn. Things went off as planned. Although the staff were upset with the plan, they understood the value of getting paid on time and not losing jobs. Things seemed to stabilize, although the downturn was still, and with no signs of any change. Business was tough, as clients were also facing the same issues.

One day, Jha ji made a request to my assistant to meet me. I had no idea why he wanted to see me. I had always wanted to give him something, a small gift—a pen. I was sure he would like it. I quickly put the pen on the table with a file atop it so that it could not be seen by the visitor. It would be a surprise for him. He knocked on the door and, with a disarming smile, greeted me. He spoke hesitantly, 'Sir, I have a favour to ask of you. I have a daughter who has done her BE in Computer Science, would you be kind enough to refer her for a job to another MNC? I know you have a lot of contacts, Sir.'

It was time for me to be surprised. I looked at her resumé. It was impressive. I asked him why I could not consider her for our own company. He looked at me and without hesitation said, 'Not while I am working here, Sir. I don't want my daughter to be embarrassed.' I promised to help, and in my heart I was determined to do my best. He walked away quickly. In all the meeting and the empathetic words of a security guard, I had forgotten to give him the gift. I felt lousy that I had missed doing something that was so important to me, something to hand over to him.

I was lost in thought—behind this person, there was a life beyond security checks and smiles: an aspiration for a better tomorrow for his daughter. What gift could I give him? Here I was, trying to make ends meet for the company. Yet, this resumé was important to me. I called up a couple of friends. They were most apologetic and cried off. Finally, I found someone who said he could give it a shot—a friend from a multinational. Fast forward: the girl, Shweta, turned out to be a gem. My friend called to thank me profusely for referring a 'genius', he said.

The crushing downturn abated, and there were green shoots of recovery. Things looked up. We had decided long back to take a pay cut and not let any of our employees lose their job. I was happy. Jha ji had given me a lesson at the right time in my life. He had given me the greatest gift: the gift of a purpose to life. Regardless of our circumstances, despite challenges, looking at things from the lens of optimism and keeping a brave face to keep doing our jobs in a pleasant way. Searching bags without taking away the dignity of a person, with a purpose that was beyond reproach. What a learning! What a gift! Thank you, Jha ji.

5

Of Delayed Flights, Blue Jeans and Choices

It was one of those days when everything goes wrong. I was in Mumbai and was to take an international flight to New York at night from Hyderabad. This meant I had to fly to Hyderabad and then hop on to the international flight. The meeting was supposed to be a short half-hour long and was to start at two that afternoon. As I said, it was not my day. The meeting spilled over and I was eyeing my watch, for I had to make sure I left the office in Mumbai at 3 p.m. at the latest. It seemed that it would take longer. I had texted the driver to be ready. Yes, a bit of multi-tasking is okay for someone who has to catch a flight. The meeting went well, and I did not bother with any attendant exchange of pleasantries post the meeting. I rushed to my office, where my travel bag was waiting. Now to the elevator and the long descent down from the thirty-second floor. The flight to Hyderabad was at half past five, and I had to make it to the airport in forty-five minutes.

The road to the airport was devoid of traffic, and things were going per plan.

I reached the airport only to see a serpentine queue to get to the ticket counter past the security. When I eagerly reached the counter, the attendant told me that the flight was delayed and would depart at seven-thirty that evening. It would be touch and go for me. The flight to Hyderabad lasted an hour, and I had to still get home and prepare for an international flight, which was at 1 a.m. the following day. All international flights had a three-hour rule and so, I had to be at the international terminal at 10 p.m. The attendant saw anxiety in my eyes and offered to check if there were other flights that evening.

There was one at 6.45 p.m., the attendant said, by a reliable carrier that was usually on time. I had a choice to hop on to the earlier flight and cancel my original flight, which would leave only by 7.30 p.m. I was caught on the horns of a dilemma. Should I now change to a new carrier, or should I stick to the original? How was I to know if my delayed flight would take off even at seven thirty? Though there was an option to take another flight that was leaving earlier, I was not sure it would take off on time either. It is at times like these that you must make a hard choice. It was now getting difficult to respond to her. I had to tell her quickly. She had contacts in the other carrier and was ready to buy a ticket for me. I had to let her know.

I decided that I would stick to my original decision. I would leave by the seven-thirty flight. No change. My wife used to say that it pays to quieten down, to not get distracted and to focus. I called up my wife and told her of my predicament. There was no way that I would be able to come home and then head back to the airport. I was stressed. She was calm. She said that she would pack a suitcase for the international trip. I also told her to ensure it had my passport and tickets. I did insist that I wanted her to pack a pair of special blue jeans, a pair that was comfortable for a long flight and travel. I said it had special buttons and began to hastily describe it. She is a practical woman. She asked me not to hyperventilate and that she would take care of it all. I left the matter in her safe hands.

My wife offered to come to the airport to hand the things to me. I told her to see if a reliable driver could come by. I did not want her to travel alone to the airport at that time of the night. The flight took off on time and as soon as I landed, I called my wife. She told me to contact a driver who was a regular for our family—he was waiting at the arrival gate. It was 9.30 p.m.

He had a large travel bag and a smaller tote. I opened the tote and saw my favourite jeans. Happiness. There would have been no way I could have made it home and back to the airport. Now, it was a tad early for the international connection, which was a relief. I changed in a nearby restroom and came back with a bag of used clothes. I had the blue jeans on. The passport bag was in the tote. I thanked the driver, gave him the bag that I had brought from Mumbai and asked him to drop it home. I also tipped him a little more than usual. By the way, the 'reliable' carrier's flight was delayed by two hours. I smiled. I had learnt a lesson.

Years ago, I had made such a choice. It was an opportunity to change my function altogether, as well as the company I was working for. I decided to stick with the same firm and function. At that time, I did not know if it was a good choice or not. Each time we are faced with such choices, it is another test, not of the choices we make but what we make of the choices. The test is of the mind and the strength of resolve; of what we can do in the time we have to make the adjustments and take the course of the journey. Instead of looking at the sudden changes in itinerary of the journey, enjoying the journey is a great way of putting that choice to good use. So, it is not the choice that makes the difference, it is what we do with the choices we make that makes the difference.

The blue jeans fit beautifully, with my plans ... and my journey.

6

Of Flipping Coins and Decision-Making

Uncle Krishnamurthy was a much-loved man. We used to call him Kittu Mama—a very quiet and thoughtful man. He was very popular with all the children at home. He was non-judgemental and always supported us in any way he could. He had a good word for everyone in the house. I have had very memorable times with him. My earliest memory of him is of him taking me to a candy shop in Madras to buy me peanut-and-jaggery candy, 'kamarakattu', a specialty in those days. You will not see kamarakattu in any of the malls. Not that I expect to. Like many of the things of 'those' days, the candy has not passed the Darwinian test—survival of the slickest, not the tastiest! The candy had not passed the new age Darwinian test—survival of the trendiest.

He would fuss with the shopkeeper and ask him to give us the biggest and the best. To us, he was a hero. We would swell with happiness, for we had the power of happiness in our small hands, a delicious candy, a piece of kamarakattu. We would then skip home with sticky hands and lips. My mother would admonishingly ask if we had been out with Kittu Mama. We would not respond to her. We simply looked down at the floor. How could we throw him under the bus?

Back to Kittu Mama. We used to see a lot of him during the summer holidays. He was indulgent of a lot of our wants and desires; things that we dare not ask our parents. He used to make a special candy made of a mixture of tamarind, sugar and salt. This used to be rolled into a ball the size of a marble and stuck on a toothpick. More, he taught us how to prepare it and make the perfect 'goli'. We used to walk around the house, feeling like Edison having invented something new. Such was the power of his personality. I guess we all need more of such Kittu Mamas all through our lives. One day, he died quite suddenly without a debriefing. It was heartbreaking. To many of us nephews and nieces, our hero had left us all by ourselves. It was not easy coping with the news. His memories live on, though, and in poignant ways. We remember him for things beyond kamarakattu. To many of us, he was a beacon of wisdom; he taught us in small ways and big. He would, with simple acts, such as taking us to candy shops, bring sunshine into our lives.

There are many other things I remember about my uncle. I was once caught in a decision-making bind: Do I? Don't I? It was an either-or situation when I was entering college, whether I should pick one course or the other. I was given a day to decide. I could take up Economics or Mathematics. I had done a lot of soul-searching but was still not certain. I was good at Math but was not sure what it offered for my future. What would I do after graduation? Economics was better, as I could try for the Indian public services, but there again, I was unsure if I could get past the stringent entrance exam. I prepared a list and filled two columns to compare the advantages of one over the other. At the end of all this, it was still not clear. What was clear was that it was confusing.

I resorted to the usual method of making a choice—flip a coin and see what comes up. One side would have Mathematics and the other would have Economics. That seemed easy. I tossed the coin and called heads. When it landed on my palm, it was tails. Hmm ... best of three flips, I told myself. Rats! ... Again, tails. Hmm ... best of five, I said to myself. I was on to my fourth flip. Things seemed even. This was going to be my last toss.

At the precise time when I flipped the coin, Uncle Kittu appeared from nowhere and caught the coin mid-air. He looked at me and asked me what I was doing. I told him that I was making a decision, and of course, that I was betting on best of five flips of the coin, and if I called correctly, it would show me one way.

Kittu Mama looked at me in a good-natured way and said that flipping coins was a great way to make a decision, but we need not flip it more than once. The coin would never lie, he added. He told me to flip for the last time and to call out heads or tails. I flipped the coin and it spun up in the air. I called heads and, even as the coin came revolving down, he caught it and covered it in his palm. 'What did you wish for when the coin came falling down?' He asked. 'I wanted heads, and badly so,' I said.

"Then don't look at the coin,' he said. 'It does not matter if this is heads or tails.' He put the coin into my shirt pocket. The decision-making had been done even as the coin was in the air, he said. 'The outcome of the coin flip is inconsequential,' he added. 'No more "best of three" or "best of five".'

Suddenly, it all fell into place. I wanted a desired outcome but could not decide and flipped a coin. Even as the coin was in the air, the heart knew what it wanted. That was the right answer! This was magic—what a great and simple philosophy!

Recently, I saw my son flip a coin, and even as the coin flashed in the air, I knew what I had to do ... and I remembered my late Kittu Mama.

7

Of Meaningful Chats and Meteoric Careers

He was a maverick. Correction: he is a maverick! Let us call him Madan. He was a successful sales professional working in a mid-sized IT company. He always had the zaniest ideas and would come up with something new almost on the fly. It was difficult to contain him. One day, he put in his papers. He said he was getting a much better offer—a big, fat ESOP and a salary about three times his current pay. He would be moving to a multinational. His CEO, a rockstar himself, tried his best to retain him, but to no avail. They had long chats over many cups of coffee. Nothing worked. Madan was determined to leave the firm, and all he asked was to be released with grace. As per process, he had to meet the human resources head, a new man in the firm. Nothing was expected of the HR head. It was a lost cause. Everyone was resigned to his resignation.

The HR head knew it was an uphill task trying to reason against a compelling offer. He knew that he was looking at a very talented man, an engineer he did not want to lose. But it looked hopeless. He knew that as with all things bright and beautiful, it all starts with a chat. He decided not to do the usual thing—a chat in the office cafeteria—but took Madan to a nearby coffee shop at a time when it would be nearly empty. It was modestly appointed, and was not meant for those motoring through or the impatient. The service was slow, which suited the HR head's purpose.

A dialogue is easy in normal circumstances, but this was a crucial conversation. The HR head did not have any plan in his mind; all he wanted was to listen to Madan. He asked Madan to speak of what he wanted—not from his head but from his heart—what he valued, what he wanted of life, and where he wanted to reach. The heart is where life begins and ends, anyway. He gently added that he had all the time in the world to help him make the right choice. He said he wanted Madan to succeed in his life and that was all he cared about, and he meant it. You will be surprised how opportunities spring up when you keep a willing heart and an open mind, he said.

Madan spoke about his family, his parents, and wafted into a dream-world of aspirations. He spoke in a rush for over an hour. The HR leader listened actively; he nodded and kept eye contact with Madan. He encouraged him to speak and it was, he said, not to ask him to stay, but to understand him better. It is magical to listen to someone who has so much to ask of life. At the end of a monologue, Madan challenged the leader: 'What is it that the firm can give me that my prospective employer can't?' The HR manager looked him in the eye and said the firm could give him something that no firm in the world could give him. Madan was intrigued and challenged him to even 'match the offer'. The HR leader smiled and said, 'No company in the world can give you "me".' It was Madan's turn to be silent. There was no arrogance in the voice. All the HR leader wanted to do was to make clear that he supported Madan. 'I can help you change the course of your destiny far beyond your aspirations. But I need two years of your life,' he added. Madan said that he would think it over.

One of the best ways to influence someone is to just listen to them with care and empathy. Helplessness is a stage of inaction of a weak mind, while actions abound for the brave heart. Madan's strengths and his aspirations were weighed that day against the potential of the future. Madan came in the next day and said he would be willing to listen. The HR leader told him that Madan would make a good HR professional and that he would invest in his development personally. Madan heard himself agreeing to it, although he was surprised with himself. By the end of the day, Madan had decided to stay. He went to meet the HR leader, who smiled and gently asked, 'Hey, what about that company's offer that "no one could refuse"?' They both had a hearty laugh.

Things happened in a whirl. In six months, he got seconded to the US office of the firm to take on the role of HR manager. One day, he called his leader and said he was getting bored. Not unexpected, of course! Another of those conversations ensued, Madan was gently persuaded to get some further education—the London School of Economics, no less. The HR head also added that he would provide all the testimonials that were needed. The entry criteria were tough, Madan was told. The HR leader knew that provocation was the axis of motivation for Madan. That would not be easy but not impossible; Madan could do it if he prepared enough, was the thoughtful encouragement.

Rise he did—he would. Meteorically, of course. Madan put in hard work, kept an open mind, and directed energies to build a career of choice. 'Each one has an edge; the talent edge. Just keep at it, hone it, feed it with a spot of education and a dollop of "can-do" attitude. And smile a lot,' Madan said at his homecoming in his firm. Make bold moves with confidence—really bold. Ah, the power of a meaningful conversation and the significant changes it brings, he added.

Oh, I forgot to mention: Madan is the HR director for a fantastic firm in the social media world. He works out of Singapore. The gracious Madan never forgot his HR leader. And it all started with a chat.

Hiring Right and Wrong

Hire character. Train skill.

—Peter Schutz

How do we hire? How are we hired by someone? What do they see in us? What do we see in others? How do we know that these would be great leaders tomorrow? These are delightful stories of discovering strengths in people. Some are of discovery by serendipity and some by design. Many are about how people were given a chance and how it made all the difference to them. The stories also speak of the ethics in recruiting and what outstanding candidates have done. There are stories of biases that one holds and how convictions have helped in many situations. There are stories of people who are great at this but don't ever get a chance to express themselves.

Often, hiring is about a perfect fit. It is also about biases that creep in insidiously, perhaps even unknowingly; it does happen. It happens all the time. How do we become aware of the biases that we hold? What is a good way to neutralize the biases? When we see someone, there is an instant positioning in our minds: like or don't like or neutral. Are we aware of whom we have met, their life stories and what they are up against? This brings me to my favorite part of what is important in hiring—LQ or Listening Quotient. I even call it 'Listen more, Question less', as that adds up to LQ.

1
The Steno and How to Become a GM

He was a man of diminutive height. A quiet man, whom I shall call Nags, a shortened version of Nagarajan. He had been an assistant—a secretary to the general manager of a well-known trading company in Chennai. He had travelled to Hyderabad to be interviewed for a new job at a multinational and was waiting for his turn in the imposing lobby of a well-appointed office. He looked anxious and wore a nervous smile. He was to be interviewed by S. Kumar, a GM of the big company. Kumar wanted a stenographer and typist, a skill approaching extinction in today's times. A steno would take down notes that were 'dictated' by another and then transcribe them on to paper. Today, any good software can do that with elan. Anyway, in the early 2000s, already this was a skill not easily available. There were three people who were shortlisted for the position.

At a preliminary interview briefing, a helpful recruiter suggested that Kumar should not waste time with Nags as he was not a good fit. Kumar, however, waved the recruiter away and asked to meet Nags. The recruiter now added that Nags was 'diminutive' in height and would not be suitable. Now Kumar was even more curious. At first sight, he was tempted to agree that Nags might be a wrong fit. The man's shirt in broad checks and his light-green trousers were the first surprise—not appealing at all. Kumar, however, swallowed his bias, offered the candidate a seat and asked about his education. Nags said that he had done an undergraduate programme—BSc, with Physics as his major. This was interesting—a Physics major was doing the job of a steno-typist! Nags then added that he had secured 86 per cent as his aggregate. Now, Kumar was curious. Sitting in front of him was a man who had a very good academic record but was doing the job of a steno-typist. He was uncomfortable at the thought that he himself had not got such high marks in college. He had been fortunate to have pursued his MBA, which got him a good job. He wondered why Nags had become a steno.

Upon gentle prompting, Nags spoke of his family circumstances, the need for him to take up a job quickly to support his ailing father, at a time when the only job available to him was that of a typist. He grabbed it with both hands, he said. After many years of working through the system, he had moved on to become secretary to the general manager. By now, Kumar had given up his prejudice about the checked shirt, the worn unpolished shoes, the short stature and the lack of a suave 'multinational' look. He asked Nags some more questions and was convinced of his versatility. It was a sad quirk of fate that the immediacy of a family need had come in the way of a good man's ambition. Here was an outstanding man whose time had come, felt Kumar.

'You will work with me for only a year and a half, by which time I would like to see you move on,' said Kumar. It was Nags's turn to be surprised. Kumar added that he wanted Nags to grow in the organization and that he would support Nags along the way. 'You will take on other roles in my function,' he added. Nags reached for his handkerchief to dry his eyes. Here was a man who wanted him to grow in the company! He had never seen it in his entire career. Nags joined in a month. He had to move into the city with his family from Chennai. His wife started work with another bank in the city.

Nags had a great quality about him. He was always right on the ground. He was not a person to sit at his desk and wait for the next call and be available to Kumar. He spent time speaking to people in HR operations. He prepared presentation slides for the GM. He would do a lot more than what was asked of him. Everyone trusted him, and he was the wise man on the ground who had a response for the many questions of the young new recruits. Everyone loved him. Nags was ever present, always ready to help and had earned the tag of Mr Reliable from those around him.

Kumar moved him after eighteen months and gave him a role in HR operations. Nags grew rapidly. One day, the US HR leader visited the firm. There was a presentation to be made by the talent leader. He simply passed the job to Nags, who set to it with gusto. A neat presentation deck was prepared. Kumar was impressed. When the HR leader came in from the US, Kumar simply asked Nags to lead the presentation, something that had never been done. Kumar had faith in Nags.

The visit was a success. Nag's presentation was a super hit. He could not speak the Queen's English. Who cared! Nags came in for high praise from the US leader. Kumar just basked in the glory of Nags. He had cultivated some skills in his protégé, all of which came in handy. Time went by.

Almost ten years later, Nags went to Kumar's house, pressed an envelope into his hand and said that he had an external opportunity and wanted his views. It was a job offer from a very reputed company for the post of 'GM–Operations'. Nags was a senior manager, but it would take him a good six years to get there in his current company. Kumar was ambivalent—should he let Nags go? He then remembered the green pants and checked shirt that he had worn to his interview. Here was Nags in a spotless white shirt, polished shoes and a smile. What a distance Nags had covered! It was the turn of Kumar to reach for his kerchief. He just hugged Nags, and they had a cup of coffee.

A secretary to a general manager was now a general manager! What a movement, what a journey! There are many in the world who need but an opportunity and a little faith. Faith in the abilities of an 'ordinary' steno-typist.

2

The Man Who Hired His Boss

I knew a certain Thomas who wanted to move out of his firm. He was not happy. He had had a lot of travel on his hands. He wanted to be with his family and spend time with them. His current job did not allow him to do that. He had to travel each week to another city and had to work almost eight days a week, or so it seemed. He decided to look for something that would not involve so much travel and talked this over with his wife, who was most supportive. It would mean they could at least spend time together over weekends and, not to forget, have the evenings through the week as well.

Thomas started looking for a job in right earnest. He was good at his work and well-known. Very soon, he landed a cushy job. It was not a well-known company that was seeking to hire him, but they made a very good offer to him. Beside the generous package, it was in the city where he lived—Bangalore: a big plus. This was like a heaven-sent opportunity. He resigned from his organization. That were many who asked him to stay back, which made the situation confusing. Then, out of the blue, the firm that was seeking to hire him sent a letter to say that they were sweetening their offer with some stocks. This would fetch him good money. Suddenly, he seemed coasting along in his life after he had put in his papers. Things were looking good. All he had to do now was send his acceptance letter.

As was his nature, Thomas called up a couple of his friends to let them know about it. A gentle way to check if he was making the right decision. It happens to many: a decision is taken, but doubts persist, and so, validation comes from friends. All of them said that the offer was outstanding on two counts—one, he would not have to travel, and two, the salary package was way ahead of other firms. He then called up one of his former team members, Sheen, whose inputs Thomas had always valued. Sheen was a man with his ear to the ground and also was a straight shooter. Sheen heard him out and did not seem very enthused by the name of the firm. He did not say much, and that said a lot.

Thomas asked Sheen what was on his mind. He got a strange response: 'I don't think you are taking the right decision,' Sheen said. While all others had supported his move, Sheen was forthright. He said that Thomas needed to study the firm well before he made the choice. Thomas was adamant and said he had made up his mind and that all was good. He almost wanted to put the phone down with a perfunctory thank you. Sheen said he would call him up in a day.

Thomas did not want Sheen to call him or speak to him. You always run a risk of being persuaded when you are at your vulnerable worst. What if the persuasion led him up the garden path to nothingness? Yet, he trusted Sheen. He was worried that the current job offer would slip out of his hands—or at least his commitment to it. On the other hand, he trusted Sheen.

Sheen was not an ordinary professional. He had come up the hard way in life. He knew what was to be done and did that with a huge focus. He was reliable and enjoyed his work. His smile was infectious, as was his laughter. He was a genial man who made everyone around him feel at ease. Sheen was intuitive, with a sharp sense of right and wrong; he was not given to a lot of analysis. He believed in getting things done.

The phone rang and, as expected, it was Sheen. Thomas was starting to feel on edge. He asked Sheen why he was so persistent. He had asked for some views and Sheen had given his views, but no reasons, merely saying, 'You need to do something better,' which seemed too general. He then asked Sheen to come clean and tell him the real reason why he was not giving his reasons straight out. His vague suggestions were not helping.

Sheen started to speak and fell silent. Then he sighed. 'Thomas, you are aware that I have joined a new company, and the first job I have is to hire my boss. I think it should be you.' None of the usual 'It would be an honour for us to have you with us, and you as my boss.' Just a simple statement, 'I think my boss should be you.' Thomas had a hearty laugh. He could not believe Sheen was being so serious about things. Sheen said that it was a great multinational that he had been hired into and he liked the culture.

It was just as Thomas feared. Sheen could be very persuasive. He spoke passionately about the new firm. He did not badmouth the firm that had made the offer to Thomas; he just said that the place where he was working was a terrific one. Knowing Sheen, Thomas asked him if there was anything else he wanted to share about this new organization. Sheen said that the only fly in the ointment was that it was in another city, not in the city where Thomas lived. So, this was a bit of a problem. No, a huge problem. This would mean, all things going well, he would have to move to another city. That was not a happy situation. However, he remembered that his wife, a simple and wise woman, always said that one should always follow one's calling. So, Thomas decided to give it a try. He asked Sheen to progress the referral, and put the phone down. Darn! Sheen had once again won. Which was why he regretted speaking to Sheen.

Things moved fast and he got selected. It was an American multinational, and the leaders he met were very fine people. They were professional, warm and welcoming. He forgot all about the stocks and the money. It did not seem to matter. The only rub was that it was in another city. He called up Sheen and told him about his selection. Sheen was at his persuasive best to take the job. Thomas consulted his family and the move took place. A new city, a new culture and new settings.

I knew Sheen from the industry, and had learnt that Thomas, whom I also know, had taken the new role and moved to the new city. I asked Sheen his reason for asking Thomas to join his firm. He laughed and said, 'A known devil is better than an unknown one.' I could not stop laughing. He added that Thomas was a good man and that he did not think he had learnt enough from him.

Thomas grew in his role and did well for himself, as I knew he would. He and I have often spoken about Sheen. He was so selfless and had the courage to ask his ex-boss to join the firm in which he was working. In a way, he hired his boss.

Sheen moved on to become a leader in another firm. Leaders are not born, they are made, and each is made differently. The best of them find goodness in others and even hire them as their boss.

3

Of Silly Questions, Pigeonholes and Heroes

She was plain-looking lady, diminutive, someone you could miss in a crowd. Let me call her Ms Ashu. She talked fast and her hands spoke faster than she did, gesticulating wildly at times. She was not a person who was easily likeable. I, for one, did not like her. Neither did many others, who were given to speaking ill of her. I kept away from such conversations but could not help listening to an occasional snippet of gossip that came my way. She wanted to do business with the company that I worked for. This was many years ago—I was more hoity-toity then. I could not suffer such people and did not lose an opportunity to stay away from her. So, you can imagine.

One day, Ashu invited me over for a breakfast meeting. I winced. You know how, when you are invited by someone you'd rather avoid, the first response is to try postponing it, perhaps the following week or two weeks down the line. I was ambitious and suggested that a 'better' time would be in the coming month. She was persistent and was willing to wait for another month. Funny how time flies. The day arrived all too soon. It was the morning I had to meet Ashu.

It was in one of the hotels near the office. I went in early to make sure I could exit soon. I heard my name called loudly, and she came running towards to me. She wore spectacles that were a tad large for her. She sat down and immediately started her sales pitch. I responded by asking a question, an inane one, one that all recruiters use: 'We will get there, Ashu, but before that, kindly tell me about yourself.' This was not something that she expected. She sat back. Her eyes turned upwards, gazing into the infinite and she began.

The daughter of a government official, she had a sister who was a 'genius', did very well in class. Her mother wanted Ashu to be a doctor and made her write the exam. She did 'what she could'. And she cleared! Admission into medical college, then or now, has never been easy. I was warming up to her now. Sitting across from me was someone who was easy to speak to. She went to the medical college and returned home after ten days. Said she did not like it. Her mother 'freaked out' on her. Her mother took it to heart and did not speak to her for a whole year. She said that Ashu had broken her heart.

She then went to a 'regular' college and, of course, did well. She became the student union leader. She even brought a multinational factory to a grinding halt, for the company had terminated the services of a principal of a local school. Ashu was warned that acid would be thrown at her. She did not relent. Now, her story was really getting to be interesting. I leaned forward, forgetting that my toast was getting cold.

After her regular BSc degree, Ashu had to do 'something'. Her uncle persuaded her to write an entrance exam for admission to a leading public sector unit. As usual, she aced the exam. But she told her uncle that she did not 'fit the culture' and opted out. This time, her uncle freaked out on her. She was now in deep water. Disowned by her family, she went to the same factory that she had helped 'shut down', seeking a job. The factory manager was furious! But, kind man that he was, he relented and gave her a job in sales and marketing even though she was not an MBA.

They gave her the jobs everyone hated to do. Ashu worked hard and won each time. She moved to a larger company that asked her to do a stint in the US, taking on an assignment that was sure-fire failure for anyone who touched it. She made a success of it and said she had not known it was an impossible task.

I was now on the edge of my seat.

Ashu returned to India to set up her own company, sold it to investors and took on a CEO's job at this company. Sitting across from me was the finest example of someone who had fought life harder than any man—and with a smile. She also had two pet dogs and spoke endlessly about how she related with them.

Ashu had been fighting like a warrior in a man's world all along and never gave up. This got me thinking. It is so easy to judge someone and pigeonhole them as good, bad or ugly! I was now in open admiration for this lady. What a story! In sixty minutes, she had taught me what it is to live a life of conviction in one's goals; a shining example of never-say-die. She gave everything to a job, and then some more. She succeeded each time, for she never judged work harshly. She taught me that it is important to see beyond the apparent image. I became her fan!

To believe in oneself and carry on trying is the core characteristic of champions. To try and give an honest shot with all the power one has—that is learning how to win each time, every time. I was not sure what else was said in that meeting and forgot everything else going on around us. I had found a hero in her. I listened to the voice of the unheard and saw the unseen—it was a revelation to see a hero hidden in the pigeonhole of ordinariness. All because of asking a 'silly question' we often use: 'Tell me something about yourself,' and sitting back to listen to a story of valour—listening without any filters; listening with an intent to understand and sans bias (although this is what I had loads of, prior to her story).

She suddenly stopped speaking and said that she had not meant to share all about her life, vulnerabilities and values, what she stood for. She got up and went to the food counter. I think she went there for she wanted to be alone with herself, to come to terms with the woman of substance she was and to admit to herself who she was, all while searching for something to eat. I think that in that moment, she discovered herself.

4

The Old Interview Coordinator

He was an ordinary man doing an ordinary job in a not-so-ordinary company. I shall call him Chinmay. He was a recruitment coordinator. He was bent with age but had a sparkle in his eyes and a keenness to serve. He was going to retire in a year or two. The final interviews were at the head office, an imposing building in Calcutta (now Kolkata). He had taken us around the building and fed us with a lot of information. We were a few of shortlisted candidates from a business school of repute. We were to meet some significant people, all senior leaders at the organization. It was a British company, a leader in its league, well-respected and recognized the world over. We were all excited. The interviews were to be in the afternoon, and we had come in early as instructed. He was the person we met as soon as we came into the building. We were happy we had someone to speak to. All around us, people were too busy to notice us, so it was nice to have someone to speak to.

Chinmay da, the coordinator, was a kind man. He was encouraging and supportive, putting in a kind word of advice to each of us who had come in for the final interview. He even came up to me, adjusted the knot of my tie and stepped back to admire his work. I thanked him. He then went to a few of the others and adjusted the jacket of one, respectfully said something to a couple of my female classmates. They thanked him too. We were so glad he was with us.

Ever keen to know our background, he asked a lot of questions. A good listener, he was enthusiastic about anything we said. His last words before he escorted us to the boardroom were: just be cool and confident. Listening to him, I wondered why he would do all of this for us or, for that matter, anyone? The interviews were tough, but the interviewers were not. After the interviews were over, he asked us to be seated and ordered tea and some lovely biscuits for us.

After a few minutes, he read out a few names and asked them to follow him. He took them to a room and sat them down. He gave them what looked like application forms to fill out. A cashier was also in the room. The door quietly shut on them.

After a few minutes, Chinmay came out to the two of us remaining outside and shook our hands and congratulated us. I was confused. I asked about the people who were in the room. He was so gentle with them and had taken them to a room while we were in the corridor on a bench. He said, 'It is important to be kinder to those who were not selected, and that takes time.' We were given our travel allowance and, of course, I got my appointment letter. (That is another story.)

Many months later, I met Chinmay again at the head office. He recognized me instantly. He was all smiles and chatted happily. I invited him for some coffee, and we got talking. He said that he had worked in the firm for over thirty years. He had been promoted to his current assignment over ten years ago. It was because he could speak fluent English with a British accent, he said smilingly. I asked him about his life and his work. He swept that question aside and said gleefully, 'I knew you would be selected. I have met so many people and am 99 per cent sure who will make the cut. It is my life's work,' he added with pride. So, just spending time with people before and after an interview got him to know who would be selected?

I asked him how he managed to get this right so many times over, to know who would be selected. He said that the time spent with recruits is valuable. You get to see if someone is taking the initiative, if anyone is good at collaborating with others; you notice who is genuine and authentic and is someone who will be as good as the people in the firm, if not better, he said. Is there a formula? I asked him. He just smiled and said that it was learnt over many years of practice. I knew he was not going to give away anything to me; perhaps it was not possible, either. I did not push further.

Then, as we arose to say goodbye, he seemed to relent, gave me a confiding smile and said, 'Son, if you get a chance, always ask a coordinator for feedback about a candidate.' It was my turn to smile. I nodded my head. He must be very good at his job.

I softly asked him, 'Does your boss know about this secret?' He smiled and kept silent. I could see a tear well up in his eye as he turned and walked away. That was a long time ago.

Each job has a specialization, and people who work closely around it learn a lot. They often become experts and should always be consulted but are seldom asked. Their tasks are often seen as mundane, forgetting that God is in the details—but they can reveal a lot of insights. They are diamonds in the rough. All it takes is a genuine interest in them and to check with them. What if someone had asked Chinmay about his work and perhaps asked him for his views? After all, he would know a lot about the culture fit of an individual, as he saw many of them up close and in an environment that was non-threatening. A simple inclusion could instil a sense of ownership of their work and pride in the company. To check and to value a person's point of view regardless of where they are in the hierarchy is a value learnt over time.

Fast forward, as I set about to interview the next person, I asked the seasoned coordinator what she thought of the candidate. There was a gleam in her eyes as she started to speak animatedly. And I remembered Chinmay.

5

Taking a Chance on a Hire

It was a long time ago. The firm was growing, and it seemed that we would never tire of hiring people in the talent function (read human resources). The talent head was a unique woman. She was unconventional, and her way of interviewing was different. Each person who went through these interviews had a clear sense about themselves after her interview. But now, the talent pool of good people was drying up, and a post needed to be filled. Sally called her team and asked them to give her a few referrals for the position. She wanted someone who was sensitive, had passion and could take initiative. There were many referrals that came her way. She was intrigued by Harbir, who was different. He did not have the usual qualification of high marks in his college or even in his MBA institution. There was something about him that got Sally to ask for an interview with Harbir.

Sandeep sent in the reference. Harbir had made a request to him, and he had just forwarded his resumé to Sally, his boss. He was sure Harbir would not be called for an interview. He then made a request, a strange one: he wanted to sit in on the interview, but not be visible to the candidate Harbir, as he was his reference. Sally agreed, as the interview was going to be via video conference. Sandeep was called and asked to sit away from the camera and not to make a sound. Sandeep wanted to learn from the experience and so, was all smiles. He was keen to see what was different in these interviews by Sally.

The interview started on time. Sandeep sat at a place out of view of the camera. Sally asked Harbir, the candidate, all the questions one would normally ask: his background, his experience and, of course, the reason why he was looking at their firm for employment. Harbir was quite eloquent about his past. He admitted he was disappointed with his academic grade point index (read marks). He regretted his inability to secure better marks at his MBA institute, which was one of the best in the country. Sally dealt with him gently and went on to ask him about his passion. What was he consumed with beyond work, something that was his passion?

At this stage, Sandeep was sure that Harbir would not be selected, and it appeared that this was the sad end of the interview. Harbir started speaking about his passion for music. He spoke about how he enjoyed singing and how he had learnt to play the guitar and several other stringed instruments. He was animated in his gestures; there was a sparkle in his eyes. He spoke passionately about his music and how he used to practise and continued to do so for at least an hour or two each day. This was going to be a long conversation. Sally asked why his music was important. Harbir just smiled and said music was his life; it gave him the energy to do his tasks every day at his workplace.

Sally then asked him what he liked doing. Harbir said that he enjoyed working with people who had a sense of purpose and people who wanted to contribute to society. He spoke about how he had done a few months of work as a teacher in a school for the underprivileged. Sally was impressed. She asked him a few questions about this side of his purpose and again, it was just wonderful listening to someone who was clear about what he wanted to do. She told Harbir that he was selected and that a letter would follow. The video conference ended and Sandeep came out of his corner.

Harbir had been sure he would not be selected and was surprised, for he did not know why he got selected. Sandeep, who was in the room, was also confused. It was not a technical interview. How was he selected? Sally explained that this was all owing to the fact that Harbir was a person who had passion, had taken initiative and could be trusted. 'But what about his university marks?,' asked Sandeep. Sally smiled and said, 'Well, the marks help bring somebody to the door, but marks are not an indication of future success.'

What someone does outside their normal work hours and the passion they invest in these pursuits determine their success, said Sally. This was a valuable new lesson for Sandeep. He was glad that he was on Sally's team. He then remembered a question that Sally had asked him: 'What is your passion?' Sandeep had then spoken eloquently about his love for reading and for teaching young people, but he never realized that these qualities helped to make the professional he was at work. It was also a gentle reminder that university marks were a stepping stone but not all of the journey.

Sally had taken a chance on Harbir, who turned out to be an outstanding professional. Many people on her team were those who had needed a chance. She was also supportive of those who were to be promoted ahead of their time. She said, 'I know they will grow into their jobs. We need to help them find their true north. We need to bet on those who have special qualities of passion and drive.' She had sorted this out in her mind quite clearly. She also exhorted the leaders on her team to do likewise. Her way was different from many regular boxed-up CHROs, who ran their function by the rulebook. She would break rules and make that a policy and then break them again!

Recently, I met Harbir. He had grown in stature and was a budding CHRO in the making. I asked him about the hero in his life, someone who had made a difference to his career. Yes, he spoke about Sally.

6
Of Perception and Reality

It was a Saturday afternoon many moons ago. I had gone to interview someone for a senior marketing role at the company where I worked. The meeting was set for three in the afternoon. Our offices were normally shut on Saturdays, but they had been kept open for me that day. The interview had been scheduled for the afternoon, for it was the only time that was available to the candidate. Yes, it was as hard in those days as it is now!

It was a bore. I was the only one in the office except for the receptionist who had been told to stay back. I could not even ask for tea or coffee, and they did not have vending machines in those days. I was walking up and down the lobby and, after a few turns, told the receptionist to call me when the candidate arrived. She was sulking and did not hide it when she said she would. No point trying to cheer her up when I was sulking too.

I tried to read the resumé. It was all of one page. I was used to reading resumés which were at least three pages long. It seemed too short, and I discarded it. Perhaps it was to do with my disposition that afternoon—a disgruntled guy. At 3 p.m., I called up the receptionist, and she said that no one had turned up. I was getting angry and impatient. How could anyone keep me waiting! I was already forming an opinion about the person, for he was not on time. I was a stickler for time, and I could not understand what the delay could be.

A few minutes later, I went to the reception area. Still no candidate; just a man sitting there, reading a newspaper. He was unkempt and unshaven, clad in a white dhoti (a sarong-like white cloth tied around his middle), T-shirt and flip-flops. I went back to my room. I came back fifteen minutes later and again asked the receptionist if there was a visitor for me. I murmured to her that I had noticed a scruffy person sitting in the lobby. The receptionist said that she had just come back after a tea break at three and hadn't noticed. She did not care, obviously. I asked if the person had approached her. She answered in the negative.

I mustered some effort, went up to him and asked if he was waiting for anyone. He said he was waiting for the head of human resources to meet him. His English was faultless and rich. The receptionist was surprised. I looked at him and thought to myself, oh, he can even speak English and manage the language well. Not bad at all. I asked if he was Swadesh, and he said he was. He did not smile but was not unpleasant. Seemed detached. I asked him to follow me and walked briskly up ahead through an unlit corridor. The man was shuffling along behind. All that was going on in my mind was, 'Oh God, give me the wisdom not to judge him too early, too soon.' I reached my office and sat behind a big teakwood desk. Very British décor! In those days, we were indulgent to a fault. The candidate sat opposite me, and I apologized for not offering a cup of tea, as it was a Saturday and the offices were closed. Guess I wanted him to know that I was working on a Saturday. He did not smile but thanked me and said he understood.

The interview started off reasonably well and was scheduled to last half an hour, after which I could leave for home and make the most of what was left of the evening. It was not to be. I did not start off with the usual 'tell me something about yourself'; I wanted a quick exit. The gent did not fit. I was bound by a promise to myself that I would not judge too soon.

What started as a perfunctory set of questions led to a fascinating conversation that lasted a full two hours. We spoke about many things, and it was easily the best interview that I have been a part of. I was listening to a very grounded and wonderful person. At the end of it, I told the candidate that I was very impressed by him and wanted to take his candidature forward; I would get him to meet our managing director (MD). We were going to shake hands, and at that moment, he remarked, 'Strange that you have not asked me about my attire.'

How was I to tell him that it was the most intriguing part of the meeting? Without waiting for me to respond, he added that he was coming from the cremation ground, having laid his beloved uncle to rest. He had had no time to go home and change, as wanted to be on time, and had rushed to the interview. He said that he was particular about time and that he had come to the reception but did not see anyone—the receptionist had arrived moments before I came there. He also added that he was very touched that I had not asked him about it. He said that regardless of the outcome, he would stay connected. He bid me goodbye and left.

How could I tell him that it was a great lesson for me? I had formed a negative opinion about him as soon as I saw him and mentally decided that he would not make the cut; I had judged him way ahead of the interview, based on what I saw. But the long walk in the corridor and the promise to myself to not prejudge had helped. Between perception and reality is a fight in the mind that is already made up, the result depending on whether one is willing to be open to new experiences. If the gates of perception were to remove their filters, we could perhaps see more clearly. Perception is skin-deep, while reality is at the heart of the matter. He did not care about his costume; he was focused on doing the right thing of keeping time. And I was bothered about his footwear!

A small detail—I still keep in touch with S., who is CEO of a very large company today. A smaller detail—he was from a top B-school in India, something I noticed after I re-read the resumé. And last detail—he did accept the job that we offered. Turned out to be our good luck.

7

A Wrong Hire and a Lesson Learnt

It was one of those difficult decisions to take. The candidate sitting before us seemed exceptional at his work and had other interests in his life. He was also an artist. We had seen a good number of people leave us in the early part of their career, and I wanted to make sure we hired right. Shyam came with great credentials. He was in the top percentile of his class and had done well in his exams. He was very certain that he would be selected; a bit cocky, I thought. My fellow panelist, Krishna, was more confident than I was about selecting him. I was a bit wary. I was unsure about his commitment to working, as he said his passion was painting and that he spent a lot of time at the easel. At one stage, he even said that he was ambivalent about his future as a software engineer. I had a quick chat with Krishna, and he convinced me to hire Shyam.

Six months after Shyam started work, I received a call from the business manager of the unit to which Shyam was assigned. He said that Shyam was not shaping up and that his commitment was lax. I feared the worst. I had anticipated it but had not been convincing in my arguments with Krishna. I told the business leader that everyone needed a second chance and that he should speak to him and give him some coaching. They were young and some needed a gentle nudge, I added. I also told him that I would meet Shyam, which I did.

Shyam looked at me and said that he had made a mistake when he came into the world of such work, which needed an interface with a computer, with painful coding all day long. He told me that he was going to take up painting in a focused way. I tried to persuade him to stick to his work. He looked at me as if I was from another planet and did not understand his position. The next day, Shyam resigned from the firm. I was most upset. It stayed on my mind for some time. I could never forgive myself for a wrong hiring decision.

Travel broadens the mind, they say. I was at Hyderabad airport when I met this gentleman. Let me call him KR. Hair neatly knotted behind his head with a rubber band. Beard left carefully untrimmed. A T-shirt that had seen a lot of the world. He smiled when I joined him. I asked him what he did. He said he was directing a movie. I was surprised. KR said it was his dream. He did not want to make it a profession, he added hastily: he would direct only two movies in his life.

This was beginning to be interesting.

What would KR work on next? He said he did not know. And where would he find money? He smiled. He needed just enough to survive, he said. He was going to paint. He was also into some natural farming, just to understand nature and to work to her rhythm, he said. All self-taught, he added, like when he tried out sand art. He had seen it somewhere and was curious about it. He had experimented on his own, used the right sand, set up the system of lights, etc., and practised it till he got it right. The skill of his hand was an added element but it did not start there, he said in all modesty. All that his mind conceived, his hands produced.

He had also tried his hand at writing and had written a book in Telugu. The English translation was coming up, he said. The book was about 'nothingness'. He was born into a rich family that lost all its wealth when he was twelve years old. They just about survived in one of the servants' quarters on their former jagir (estate). With a broad grin, he said, 'My parents gave me nothing.' It turned out to be a boon. He did not have to stay attached to family money. He loved his dog, Dolly, who was his only possession. He learnt a lot from her. He had spent four years of his life doing nothing. Just nothing. He said to his mother, 'If you can feed Dolly and not expect anything from her, I expect the same from you.' His mother just smiled. This nothingness helped him to meditate on life and what he wanted—just 'to be', not focus on 'to become'.

What sort of work would he do? He said he would do something that captivated his mind. We often mix work and value. Work and pay are what play in our mind. Take a painting. That was not regarded as work! And yet, when we purchase it, it would be called a 'work' of art. To him, it was just an avenue to allow him to 'be'. Work, he said, has been made to look like it should be laborious and serious. Enjoy what you do, and it will no longer be work. Experiment with a curious mind, and it will no longer be work. Delve into your being, and work will no longer be onerous. Express yourself with freedom in what you do, and then it would not be work.

His parents gave him nothing. And that was far more than something. And, in turn, the conversation gave me nothing and yet something. Follow your passion beyond the template of success, and satisfaction follows. Pursue your dreams to the road less travelled, and you will discover your edge. KR was an aspiring engineer from a fine university, lost his way, discovered himself, and became a celebrated artist in perhaps the most unconventional medium—sand art!

Our flight was announced, and I parted from KR when I was lost in the wonderment of the conversation. I had learnt so much in that short time. KR taught me a lot. KR—yes, Kanti Rasa—India's foremost sand artist today. Play to people's strength. My mind moved to the wrong hire in Shyam. I was positive he will be a great artist one day. I no longer carried the guilt of a wrong hire. I just picked up a great lesson along the way.

Recognition

There is more hunger for love and appreciation in this world, than for bread.

—Mother Teresa

Recognition has a lot to do with encouragement and how that has propelled others to excel. The act of showing respect to one who has gone above and beyond the norm is very uplifting. People make sacrifices to support others. There are no medals to be won, and yet they do it. It is truly inspiring. Ultimately ,what matters is the outcome for an organization, but for the many people involved, it is about what happens to them and what is the rub-off on others. It is also about culture-building; a certain focus on that which is often forgotten: an acknowledgment.

My father had a particular trait. Wherever he went, he would take a moment to thank anyone who rendered a service. As a child, I had seen it in him. He said he had learnt it from his father. I am never sure if I could be as good as he was. It did seem important to him. He was a much-loved man; a giver. Perhaps it was more to do with what he could do so easily: find something good in everyone he met. Recognition does not cost much, he used to say. It does cost a lot if it is missed, he would add wryly. I never understood these things growing up. Now, I do. Can I find something right in someone, at least once a day? Some days, I do; some days, I struggle. I try.

1

Of Pencils and Recognition

I can never forget my teacher, Ms Prema, whom I have recalled elsewhere in this book. Many years ago, my father was transferred from Calcutta to Madras, as these places were called then. As it was in the middle of the school year, I had lost six months of school. I joined fourth grade and worked hard to keep pace with the others. Mid-term exam results were upon us, and the dreaded day came when the class teacher would read out all our report cards. I was new and quite sure that I would have failed in my exams. The demands made on us were big, and I was trying to make sure I passed the exams.

Ms Prema was our class teacher. She was a strict teacher, but a kind one, pleasant of demeanour. She liked a bit of drama and made it a point to make a short speech in anticipation of the prizes. The toppers got shiny trophy cups and a certificate of merit. She also had a few books on her table—consolation prizes, meant for those who were the 'also-rans'. Ms Prema called out our names, and to each one she said some words of encouragement. She did not miss out anyone.

Then came the dreaded few who had failed in the exams. She patted them on the back and asked them to study harder. It was done with such amazing grace! Even those who failed received their report card like a prize.

My name was called out at the end of the list, as I was new to the class. I trotted up from the last row in the class to her desk. With a flourish, she handed me a green pencil and said, 'I am sure you will do much better in the coming days. This is for your efforts.' She patted me on my back. To anyone, it would seem quite ordinary. Here was a teacher who wanted someone to do well. She wanted to hand out something and handed out a green pencil. What was different was that this pencil was a used pencil.

The moment was special—while other students were given a trophy and a certificate, I was given a used pencil stub. But that was priceless. That pencil till date remains the single most memorable recognition in my life. It left a deep impression on me for a reason: it was my teacher's way of reposing faith and trust in me. To the toppers, it was an acknowledgment of an achievement; to me, it was to cheer me on. How many did I have in my life who cheered me on! My marks were ordinary; nothing to speak about. And yet, the pencil was important.

Years passed, and I got married. I remember my wife had cooked us our first meal. I had hardly had my first morsel when she asked me how it was. I smiled and said it was the most wonderful food I had ever had and added that it was much better than my mother's cooking. A white lie. It's a different matter that my mother was not around. It was a terrific moment of bonding. I felt great, and she felt as if she had won Master Chef. In that instant, I realized that both the giver and the receiver feel wonderful. Voila! This is so important.

Recently, I went to visit a colleague at her workplace. It was festooned with certificates and trophies. I asked her what was the most prized one in that lot. She picked, from among all her prizes, a handwritten note given by her boss. Priceless, she said. That piece of paper mattered the most, as it was a real token of appreciation of her achievement, albeit small. He had come over to her desk and personally pinned it on her board, she said. I could see pride in her eyes, that special moment of joy that she was reliving. The paper had seen better days, the words were fading and quite invisible. And yet, it was important to my colleague. To her, this was precious.

This morning, I went to the badminton court to meet someone. Many of my colleagues were there, playing. They invited me to play. I had never played badminton; I was never good at games. I started timorously, but each time I was able to return the shuttle, there was much applause and encouragement. By the time I left the court, I was feeling like a champion. I wished I had many of such members around who would add a small dollop of goodness. Recognition is like oxygen; a life-giver. Everybody needs it. People work in organizations, but they stay because there is someone who cares and values what they do.

I realize that all of us need appreciation. Even bosses need it. As do your spouse, children and other family members. Anyone. Social media cracked the code and added the 'like' feature (and not a 'dislike' one). Small wonder we turn to it, for there are many out there who care to 'like' what we post. People take our words seriously. Small acts of kindness go a long way. We tend to find faults easily. Can we catch people doing something right? In that moment, it can be life-changing. For these are the moments that matter and show that you care.

That day, long ago, Ms Prema taught me to recognize and appreciate anyone I care about, even just once a day. Your spouse, colleagues, friends, relatives—all need a hug. Even a virtual hug will do. Think what your call meant to that old aunt that you almost forgot, or to your long-lost friend who once made a difference to your life. This morning, I remembered the green pencil stub from Ms Prema: it brought me a smile.

2

Of Affection, Appreciation and Gratitude

I left for my morning walk and approached a park. It was some distance from my house, and it was special, for it had a few peacocks and many birds. There were plenty of trees and a lot of people walking around. Some sat on tastefully designed benches. Alongside the park was a very busy road. I reached the park entrance and purchased an entry ticket. I was about to move past the turnstile gate when, out of the blue, a child ran from the park and on to the busy road where cars were whizzing past. I had my heart in my mouth. I thought that it was the end of the child. The mother came running from the park towards the child, who thought it was a game and ran faster into the oncoming traffic. Then, he realized his peril and froze in fright. Suddenly, a man appeared from nowhere and scooped up the child, just in time, and laughed heartily. The child screamed with joy, 'Dad, you saved my life! You are the best father in the world.' That was father–son bonding at its best. Whew! No chiding, no shouting; just two souls in a bond of affection—precious, timeless. The mother, standing beside them, had tears in her eyes. I was stumped seeing all this unfolding in front of me.

I returned home after the walk. We sat down to have our morning tea. My neighbour dropped in with his daughter, Priya, a youngster who had secured admission at Indian Institute of Technology. My wife congratulated Priya and sang her praises. I added to the conversation and congratulated Priya. My neighbour said that it was not a big deal and had a scowl on his face. Clearly, he was downplaying her achievement. Priya, looking a bit under the weather, said a perfunctory 'thank you' and ran off. My neighbour left shortly thereafter.

The afternoon brought us unfortunate news. A good friend and a mentor of many years had passed away after a brief illness. He was not all that old, just sixty-three. He was someone I admired; a man who had a deep sense of values and believed in caring deeply for others. I had spent a lot of time with him just listening to what he said. Each time he spoke, it was education of a high order. I wish I had written down all of what Mahesh had said. Yes, this was Mahesh as in V.S. Mahesh, a very well-known HR professional of yesteryears. I shared the news of his demise on Facebook and wrote a few lines about what V.S. Mahesh meant to me. I shared the note on other groups. I had not met him in a long time. I felt guilty that I had not expressed my regard and respect for him and told him what he meant to me. The note I posted went viral. There was a flood of responses—eulogies from people, talking about what a wonderful man he was. This went on for a long time. We captured our thoughts on a page, which we sent to his family later that week.

Later in the evening, I remembered all that had happened that day, three events: one of someone saving his child's life, another of a father downplaying the achievement of his daughter, and lastly the guilt of someone who wished that he had expressed sooner his adulation and respect for his mentor. I realized that over time our propensity to express our affection for someone goes down. Our appreciation, our gratitude and the ability to express what people mean to us go down over time. It is almost as if it does not exist. Perhaps we think it is not needed, perhaps we wait for the perfect day to say it. It also dawned on me that as one grows older, they all return—the expressions of joy, gratitude and praising someone. I had seen them in grandfathers and grandmothers. A grandparent's unbridled love of their grandchild, their ever-forgiving nature, their ability to put things in perspective and to live life to the fullest. They discover something that they missed out as parents, expressed love, no holds barred ... Small wonder, grandparents are loved the world over.

It all came back to me. The day was teaching me something. The child taught me unconditional love. The danger notwithstanding, the father was all joy when the child was saved. Another thing, I am sure Priya would have loved to be acknowledged by her father for getting admission to IIT. Lastly, Mahesh taught me to live in the present, and perhaps I should have reached him much before. What is the use of praising someone when he has departed the world?

I went to the kitchen and noticed that the kitchen counter was a mess. My wife was cooking something new. Something that I had not seen before. I tasted the food, and it was divine. I told her that the food was made for the gods. She made a face implying that she did not believe me. In a minute, there was a question to me: 'Tell me, is it really that good?' I answered with all sincerity that it was. She was smiling. Not used to compliments, I guessed.

I moved to the room where my son was studying for a college examination. I complimented him on his wonderful handwriting and his great memory. He smiled, and his face lit up. I called up my friend of many years, and we had a long chat. I told him that he was a tower of strength to me and how, in my darkest hours, I thought of him and how he always had an answer to the questions I posed to him. He was puzzled by my call, but thanked me nevertheless.

Can I perhaps catch someone doing something right each day? Can I appreciate someone once a day? Can I let my friends know what they mean to me? And express gratitude to people who made a difference, in my life while they are still around? Maybe one should start right away? Perhaps it is time to call one's aunt or uncle, dad, mom or a friend, anyone! Let them know what they mean to you and why. I am sure V.S. Mahesh would have loved to hear what we thought of him; no, what I thought he meant to me.

3

A True Friend at Work

He seemed like any other person at work. Let me call him Anand. He was a man who worked selflessly and was liked by many for his brand of friendship, which was non-intrusive. He never asked anything from anyone and was always available. We called him the connector. He knew everyone in the office and beyond. If you asked him for anything, he could get that done for you. If you wanted to reach anyone, he could easily connect you to anyone anywhere. He did this in the nicest of ways and did not wait to be thanked. He was direct and subtle at the same time. Great qualities. He was not a party man and seldom attended any, and kept away from public glare. Yes, if you invited him personally and asked him in a nice way, he would attend. He was a good friend. He would keep confidences, be available to speak to, and if you wanted to vent something, he would lend a listening ear. Personally, he would keep to himself, though. That was Anand.

He had joined the firm a few years back and was known to be a quiet man. He smiled a lot and was very thoughtful. He did small things that made him special. The secretaries loved him. He cared about them. A nice note on their table to brighten the day. A special note to someone who had a new born in their home. He had special cards that he made himself. He used to pass one to each of the staff. What was special was that he knew exactly what each one wanted. For some, it was encouragement; some needed a dash of smiles; and for many, just the plain hope of a better tomorrow. He was not high up in the hierarchy but was not way down the ladder either. He was a senior manager. Funny how everyone thought of him as their own friend.

His own life was an open book. Everyone knew him to be a good singer. A good help at home to his mother, and to his wife an adorable husband. His clients loved him. He was always available. He had two small kids, and they were the love of his life. He had a picture of his wife and kids on his desk. A happy family. He always seemed to be in control. You could raise your voice against him, and he had a calm way of responding. Almost Buddha-like. He had his failings, of course. He was not good at speaking in public and would not take the centre stage even if you asked him to. He would always be on the sidelines and took care that he would not be the person in the spotlight. I was introduced to him one day by a senior colleague when I joined the firm. All he said to me was that Anand was a good man whom he had never understood. I did not understand this comment, but it stuck to me in a strange kind of way.

I was working late one day—one of those days where one had to finish things no matter how long it took. I did not want to take work home. I would stay at the office and knew it was going to be a long evening. It was a Friday, and I had ordered some food early that afternoon. Everyone had left. The work would not stop. It was a long night. There was so much to do. Around four in the morning, I decided to call it a day, or should I say night. As I moved to the door of the floor, I saw Anand in his cubicle. I had not expected to see him. Must be that he was burdened with some heavy-duty work. He smiled and asked if my work was done. I laughed and told him that work was like waves on the shore—ceaseless.

I then asked him what had kept him so long. His response shook me. He said that he was waiting for me to finish up and wanted to make sure he was around in case I needed any help. 'But I didn't want anyone to wait for me! I did not ask you to wait for me, Anand,' I protested. He said that it did not matter. The best part was that Anand was not even from my function and had nothing to do with any work that I did. He just did not want to leave me all by myself. He said this to me lightly; he did not make it seem like a big deal. I gave him a warm hug, and my eyes all but moistened. I thanked him profusely. He cared about me.

I escorted him to his bike, and he left soon after. As I started my bike to head home, Anand stayed on my mind. He had waited just to make sure that I had some support: a true friend at work. He did this without my asking. No fuss, no long speeches. He did not even wait to be thanked. It reminded me of my mother, who stayed up many a night when I was studying for my exams. What a man! Could I even be a tenth of this man? I reached home, entered my room and, given it was too early to wake up and too late to go to sleep, just lay staring at the ceiling, thoughts a-buzzing. There are many who are around at work, who put in their might in a selfless way, not even caring if they are recognized for it or not. Many things get done at work owing to such people. They bring much-needed support to people who may not even reach out to seek help. They are available for any conversation, and perhaps a few are like John Milton's proverbial 'They also serve who only stand and wait'. There are many like Anand—a true friend at 'work'. Inspired, I told myself that I hoped to be one. To somebody.

4

Of Routine Matters and the Gift of Life

He was but an ordinary guy doing an ordinary job in an ordinary company. In the course of his work, Joe—let us call him that—had many requests and applications coming to him, and in some he had to weigh in with his views. All good. Many were about loans to be sanctioned, and some were about making some exceptions. All very routine. He did what he could in his ordinary way to address each of these on merit. No one even looked in his direction after a loan was sanctioned. They were not required to, in any case.

One day, an ex-employee, Ram, called him. He said it was the eighth birthday of his daughter and asked Joe to be there, for it was an important event. Joe usually found some excuse to extricate himself from such events. He found them boring, and he was a loner. He would have to pick up conversations, and that was not his forte. Ram was persistent; he visited Joe at home and told him a few things about his life over the past four years since he had left the city. He reminisced about many things, including a loan. Joe looked at him quizzically. Ram said that he had once applied for a medical loan for his daughter, who was in critical condition in hospital. The loan application had come up to Joe for approval. The amount was twice what Ram was eligible for; something that had never been approved before.

Joe had cleared it, he said. He had added a small postscript: 'as a special case', just in case this came up for questioning by the auditors. He asked Joe if he remembered this case. Joe was quick to respond, 'No, I don't remember.'

Ram then told him that he owed his daughter's life to Joe's timely action. He had been running from pillar to post when he had approached Joe with the request and was pleasantly surprised that the loan amount was approved. He had explained the situation to Joe, and after that he had seen Joe writing something on the application. It was an approval that was not in line with the company policy. Joe mumbled that he had no recollection and said that the meeting was over. Ram was persistent and thrust an invitation card into his hands and went away. Not before thanking him all over again.

Joe sat back and thought about the number of cases he had handled in all his routineness. A small act of approval of a loan, with a small application of mind, had saved a life! It was not an ordinary job after all! An act of great kindness is one where the giver does not know it and the receiver does. If this is what a routine job could do, look what he could have done with application of mind, he thought.

Joe was lost in his world of ordinariness of what he should take as a gift for Ram's daughter. She had already got the gift of life.

5
A Faded Note and Purpose

Rishi passed by the desk of Anita, his colleague, on his way to the coffee-vending machine. Anita was not at her desk. She kept a clean desk, no papers around. No books and fancy personal belongings, toys and the like. Her pin board was spotless, with a to-do list. There was also a faded 'thank you' card. He went on to get his coffee. There, he met a colleague and got chatting and ended up spending some time with her speaking idly about things. He was feeling low, and his time with his colleague helped lift his sagging spirits. He had wanted to speak to Anita, but as she was not at her desk, he had moved to the coffee machine in the hope of meeting someone to speak to. Work kept him long at the office and on the rare 'work-from-home' days, he still worked as hard. He never felt appreciated, and perhaps that got him to feel low about his job.

Rishi went back to his desk and, with a sigh, started his work. It was going to be a long day. He opened his mails and saw one from Anita to say that she heard from a colleague that he had come by her desk. He smiled. He decided to walk across to her to have a word or two. It was just diagonally past the workstations, a short walk across the large, imposing office.

Rishi met Anita, and the first thing she asked was, 'Is all well? you seemed to be stressed about something.' He had not anticipated this. He thought he kept a calm and neutral face all the time. He mumbled that all was well; he just wanted to have a chat with her. 'Nothing in particular,' he added. Anita seemed to read his mind and everything about him. She looked at him, complimented him on his presentation slides that he had prepared for his manager and said that they were so much on point. It brought a smile to his face.

Rishi asked Anita how she always seemed so very happy and composed. She just smiled. He was now inquisitive. Anita and Rishi were good friends, and he could say anything to her. He opened up with 'I have known you to be grumpy and terse; you used to keep to yourself. What made the change in you?' Anita smiled and, with a dreamy look on her face, said that one manager changed her outlook. She looked at her softboard and pointed to a faded card on which something was written. She said that the card made a big difference to her and even saved her marriage. Now, Rishi was curious. 'Would you mind sharing more?'

Anita said that she had had a difficult year with a lot of things happening on the personal front, and it reflected on her work, too. She was diligent but she could not hide her emotions, and they came to the fore at all the inappropriate times in large meetings. She worked hard, but everything seemed to go wrong. Her manager had changed; a new manager had come in his place. This one was a strict disciplinarian and was always in a hurry, demanding more than it was possible to give. Anita did her best to please. One day, her manager wanted her to prepare a presentation deck for the leadership. Anita had no idea how to start and or to even present the topic. She asked for help from one other person who knew how to prepare a presentation deck. She put her thinking cap on and started work.

She was so absorbed that she forgot to cook that evening. Her husband had come home, and he was at his acerbic best. Things were not going well between them, and it was only a matter of time, Anita had felt, before the end came. She did her best to tell him that her work would be over in no time. He was insistent that she prepare food that instant. Anita lost her cool, and things escalated to a point of no return. Anita said nothing, just picked up her laptop and a travel bag with a couple of clothes, and with tears in her eyes, just walked out on him and to her friend's house. She put her phone on silent mode to avoid any calls from her husband. James was not a bad chap; it was just that between two working professionals, it was difficult to find the time needed for them to talk things through. It was a difficult night, and she did not sleep well.

The presentation slides went to her manager. Anita was called to explain her point of view. She did so, and with conviction. Her manager was all ears and egged her on with searching questions. The meeting ended. Anita left the cabin, unsure of how she had fared. All she knew was that she had given her best. Her thoughts went to her husband, who must have felt really upset with her. She did not know how to deal with this situation and was scared of asking anyone.

With this dilemma on her mind, she left her work desk to have a cup of coffee at the vending machine.

As soon as she came back, she noticed an envelope on her desk. Nothing very fancy. She opened it and found a plain card with the following lines on it: 'Anita, thank you for a wonderful contribution to the firm. You do an outstanding job in anything that you take up. Keep up the great work. Sincerely so.' She was elated, she said to Rishi. She had thought she was average; now her manager had written her a nice note. She went to the manager's cabin to thank her and tell her how much this meant to her. Her manager simply said to her, 'You did a great job. Now find something good in someone, at least once a day.' Anita left the cabin and went back to her desk.

She then re-read the lines on the card. Guilt pangs enveloped her. Was she so good at her marriage? She immediately called James for a quick meeting at a café nearby. She rushed into his arms and could not hold back her tears. James was ever so thoughtful, and she had never once appreciated him. They went home together that evening and never looked back, she said.

At work, 'catching someone doing something good once a day' was her mantra. Her purpose, to make the world around her a better place. She pointed to the card. The words were faded, but imprinted on her mind. Her job was to pay it forward. Rishi looked at Anita and said that it was the best day of his life and added, 'Anita, you are a great teacher,' and both hugged each other for fear their eyes would say more in that poignant moment.

6

Of Caring, a 10K Run and Winning

It was one of the company-sponsored running events: a 10K run, promoting health through running and the idea of getting employees to be more aware of their physical well-being. It was a fun Saturday morning in January that the whole organization used to look forward to. Many hundreds used to participate in it. The preparation for the event used to begin many days in advance. There were whole teams who were on the job for at least a couple of months. Managing the nominations for the event was itself a huge effort. You then had the monograms and the banners, the permissions. Easily one of the larger projects that was handled by the firm.

Mark was one of the more seasoned runners. He had practised for over a month for the event and wanted to make sure that he was in the top ten runners. He had timed himself. A college athlete, he was confident. He was doing well. All he had to do was get a little warmed up before the event so that he could get straight to the running and show people a thing or two about what it was to run a race. He was sure that many came just to run and have their pictures taken at the finish. They were not serious runners. He was one. Yes, he was a tad arrogant—and why not. He was good.

The running track was the road around Hussain Sagar Lake in Hyderabad. Regular traffic on that day would be diverted, and the traffic police was in full swing to regulate the cars on the road. It was a picturesque run around the lake, with coloured flags all along the track. There were balloons and festoons of buntings too. The Buddha statue in the middle of the lake added a touch of grace to the scenery.

The time was 5.30 a.m. when the referee was to fire his pistol in the air to signal the start of the race. Mark had 'warmed up' about ten minutes prior, in readiness for the race. However, the race was waiting for the chief guest, and he was nowhere to be seen. The runners were getting restless. There was a nip in the air, and Mark felt his body getting cold. Suddenly, without warning, the referee fired in the air and there was a surge as the runners took off, as did Mark. Something unusual happened as he felt a cramp in his calf muscles and just sank to the ground. Other runners ran all around him. He felt miserable. Just then, a hand reached out and helped him stand up. His friend asked him to put his arm around his shoulder. All Mark could do was limp. Running was out of question.

His friend said, 'Let us just limp to that red flag ten metres away. Keep your hand on my shoulder.' Mark was in pain but held out. His friend then said that they could hobble to the yellow flag, ten metres ahead, and they did just that. And then to the blue and then the orange; the unknown friend gently asked him to get to the black flag—this time, on his own. Mark forgot his pain and started to heed his friend. All he wanted was to keep his focus on getting to the next flag, reach that flag, and then look for the next flag up ahead. It was a mind game. It was tiring. He remembered his friend. Almost as if his friend was wanting to tell him that he needed to break up his ten-kilometre running goal into small, manageable steps and focus only on one of them at a time. His pain seemed to be a lot less now.

In his mind, Mark also remembered that 'a journey of a thousand miles starts with a small step'. All he wanted to do was to run to the next flag coming up on the road ahead. It seemed easy now. He had to run to the next flag. Simple. And so, he ran with a vigour beyond compare. There were people all around him, many running with him, others cheering him from the sidelines. He searched for his benefactor, but he was nowhere to be found. He decided to focus on the work at hand—to run. He kept pounding the asphalt, without a break in between. It was hard and yet easy, for all he had to do was to reach his next flag. But he was getting more confident with each passing flag.

About forty-seven minutes later, he found himself breasting the tape at the finish line and sinking in a heap. People gave him water and fussed over him. They got him to stand, and he kept walking around to get his breath back. The organizers milled around him, and one of them told him that he was one of the top ten runners. His friend was nowhere to be seen. He waited for him to complete the race. He waited in complete wonder at someone who cared so much for him that he forgot his own need to succeed. A few minutes later, his friend, his hero, arrived at the finish line.

They shared a warm hug. Mark smiled and those around did not notice the tears in his eyes, easily mistaken for sweat. The much-awaited celebratory event was coming up. The chief guest had arrived. The presentation ceremony of the medals was going to take place. Names were called to huge rounds of applause. Mark's name was called and he went up to take his medal. The clapping was deafening. In his heart, he knew that it was Anupam Lal, his friend, who had won. He deserved the medal much more than he did.

Mark learnt much more that day. In winning, there is always a guiding hand and a winning heart. There were sacrifices others made for him to succeed. Actions and words that egged him on, made him give his best, and recognized that he could make it through to the finish.

Mark walked across to Anupam, hung the medal round his friend's neck by its colourful ribbon, and they all had a hearty laugh. Each one knew who the winner was, but only he, Mark, knew who the real winner was!

7
The Dentist's Consulting Fees and Kindness

They were driving back from the temple, an old mother and her son. She wanted a pill that would kill her toothache. He felt it best to get her a dental check-up. She was worried that it would cost too much and, in any case, she was waiting to be called by her Maker, as she put it. Why waste money, she said, much to his chagrin. She did not want to be a burden to her son; he would need all he earned in the days to come. She had lived a full life, she used to say. Her husband had passed away a long time ago, and her son was looking after her. She was fond of her son—he was the one she cared for most in her life.

They saw a dentist's signboard on the way. It was a modest clinic and didn't seem good enough for his mother. She, however, decided that it would do.

He held her hand and walked her in. It was a clean place, with a cheerful but tired-looking receptionist in the waiting room. She asked them to wait. It would not take long, she added. The place was milling with people, young and old.

The receptionist called out the son's name. He was surprised. They had not been in the queue long enough. It must have been in error, but he did not complain. It meant his mother would not have to wait for long He accompanied her along the short corridor, and they entered a smallish room that had a young, smiling man for a dentist. Rare, he thought. He carefully assisted his mother into the dentist's chair. The dentist asked the patient several questions in English. The son carefully translated the dentist's questions into Hindi, the language they spoke at home. He translated his mother's answers for the doctor, speaking in a soft voice. They were told of a certain procedure that had to be done as soon as possible, that it would not take too long and that it would not be painful at all. Her tooth had to be extracted.

The son patiently explained this to his mother. It was clear that the offending tooth had to be removed. At first, she protested vigorously, saying that it was not needed and would cost a lot. Her son was a tad embarrassed and hoped the others in the waiting room had not heard her speak about the expenses. He gently told her that he was earning enough to pay for a doctor's consultation and minor procedure. He had to raise his voice a bit, as she was hard of hearing. The mother understood and nodded smilingly. They left the clinic. The following morning, the tooth was extracted. Almost routine stuff. The old lady was asked to sit at the reception for a bit.

Meanwhile, the dentist asked the son to meet him in his office. He told the son, 'I could not sleep last night, and you were the reason. The way you held your mother, the way you treated her, your gentleness, was not lost on me. My wife, the receptionist, noticed it as well. When I was going to retire to bed, she asked me, "Hey, do you treat your mother like that man in the clinic today? And will you treat her as well when she is old and infirm?" I have a mother and I am not sure if I have treated her the way you do.'

The dentist went on: 'As if that were not enough, my pregnant wife felt her stomach and asked me, "Will the child inside me treat me in the same way when I am old and hard of hearing?"'

Care is a matter of the heart in action. Elders need care the way infants do. The son was clearly at a loss of words and did not know what to say to the dentist. He smiled and nodded, held the dentist's hands, and said that he was sure that the doctor would be an even better son than him. He then left the dentist's office. On the way out, he met the receptionist and asked her what he owed for the consultation fees and the procedure. The lady smiled radiantly at him and told him that it was waived off. Paid in full by a poignant lesson learnt about elder care, she added. All his protestation could not change her mind. His mother pulled him away and nodded her head, pleasantly surprised that there were such people around.

Just then, the dentist came out of his office and folded his hands and bowed. His mother raised her hands to bless him and did likewise for the receptionist. They left. Life is beautiful. Just beautiful!

LEADERSHIP

What is the next thing you need for leadership? It is the ability to make up your mind to make a decision and accept full responsibility for that decision.

—Field Marshal Sam Manekshaw

There are more theories of leadership than about any other subject in the field of human resources. Leadership in action can be about simple things, like showing up when needed most by a team member. It can be about how to stand up for a team member, how to inspire others on a team. Do we raise aspiration in people? How do we do this? How do we instill fairness in people? Do we give our people a second chance? Do we create faith in them, and how do we get them to be our ardent followers? A leader is also a dealer in hope. How do we repay faith and support them when the chips are down?

To me, leadership is about the support that one gives to one's team members, about giving a vision for them to see the future and about making it worth their while to work at what they enjoy doing best. It's getting the best out of people by making them feel that it was their success, after all! Not all of us are like the larger-than-life heroes whom we admire as leaders; it is the everyday leader, whom we can touch and relate to, that is truly endearing. The everyday leader can exert an influence that is incredible. How do we look into ourselves and discover the leader in us? Much of work is about someone who leads, someone who follows and someone who believes they can do a better job of leading!

1

Stand Up: A Lesson in Leadership

I was positive that I was going to lose my job. Not a place where you would want to be early in your career. It all seemed so unfair. You were held responsible for something that was out of your hands.

Let me start from the beginning. I was working in a large multinational organization in their explosives factory in the heart of what was then Bihar. A well-known brand, and an organization that many aspired to work with. I was the administration officer of the manufacturing plant. As an admin officer, I was responsible for guest houses and transport. We had three guest houses, and the upkeep of the guest houses was my responsibility. As for transport, I was responsible for five cars, all owned by the company. Of course, we had no Uber, Ola or tourist taxis in those days. We had to make do with the company cars. The nearest towns were two hours away. And each time a company car went to the better-known towns of, say, either Dhanbad or Ranchi, the nearest towns, it came back and faithfully went to the garage for repairs. This was owing to the execrable state of the roads then. It was a constant battle with the garage to make sure the cars were repaired on time. They too were overwhelmed with the factory's own internal transport vehicles and their repairs.

One day, it so happened that all five cars were in the sick bay. I prayed that the garage would release at least one by the morning. It was not to be. An officer wanted to requisition a car to go to Dhanbad, and I explained that no cars were available. He was upset and said that production was at stake and I would be held responsible. I was stressed out. What was I to do? I had no cars to give him. The situation was grim. The factory superintendent, the one who had asked for the car, was no friend of mine. He said he would escalate the matter to the general manager. As expected, the GM of the factory called me to his room. It was a long walk to his office. He was known to be short of temper, and he seldom listened to anyone. Such was his reputation. I knew that I was going to be fired. I was already stressed out.

Ralhan was the superintendent of the company garage. He was a fine man; someone who knew that there was a cooking time for anything on the fire. He was helpful to anyone who was good to him. He had a reputation for being nasty as well. I knew of Ralhan and so, made friends with him. If my cars needed repairs, it would be good to have him on my side. I used to go to the cafeteria with him and have the customary tea with some snacks. We would speak about anything other than maintenance of cars in his garage. We had hit it off well. He was good to me, and that was important. I ran to him to check if any of the cars could be salvaged, as the matter was getting escalated. He took me to each of the cars just to make sure that I was not being bamboozled. It would take at least three hours before even one of the cars would be roadworthy. He told me that it was futile pressurizing his mechanics, as that would not help. He added that he would come with me to the GM to explain it all to him. I appreciated his wanting to help me.

I arrived at the GM's door. Even as I walked in after the customary knock on the door, he started to pound me without giving me a chance to explain. He would not relent. I was in a daze. The room started to look larger than I knew it to be. He did not ask me to be seated, and I was weak in the knees, even as he went on his tirade. Suddenly, the door opened without a warning and my boss, the administration manager, barged into the room and physically stood in front of me, blocking me off from the GM. I could not see the GM, for my boss stood physically in front of me. He then addressed the GM: 'While the lad is responsible, I am accountable for this failure. What can he do when all the cars are worn out? I should have budgeted for new cars. I have to run a department with poorly maintained cars. What can the lad do? He did not have a car to give to the requisitioner. Besides, I am accountable. If anything, ask me, not him.' My manager then turned to me and ordered me to leave the room. I did not wait a moment. I ran, the coward in me goading me on.

My boss returned to his room in some time. He appeared to be calm. He spoke nothing other than that it was all taken care of. I was curious to know what he had done in a situation where he had no transport for someone who needed one so badly. He turned to me and smiled. He said that he had turned in his own personal car for the job, and he patted me on my back and said that I should give him a heads-up when such things happened. My anxieties fizzled out in that moment, but I was shaken. He had given his own car for the use of the office, something that I had never seen anyone do. I was touched. I had just witnessed leadership at its best. He did not throw me under the bus but took full ownership and even gave his own car for the use of the firm. He taught me the principle of leadership: to 'stand up' for your team member in the hour of need. It would have been easy for him to advise me and even find fault with me, but he didn't. He stood up for me. I have never forgotten Capt. Arvind Nautiyal. Thank you, Captain, for giving me a great lesson in leadership—to stand up for someone on your team.

2

Learning from the Everyday Leader

We all learn from inspiring leaders. They have so much to give and so much to share about their experiences. I used to go to meet up with such people at seminars and conventions; when they appeared on TV, I would make notes of the small and big things that they said and did. Whenever I got a chance to meet someone who had succeeded against all odds, I would feel completely overwhelmed in their presence. I remember someone once said that leaders are ordinary men and women who have something that is distinct about them, and that one should learn from each of such qualities. I would leave such seminars feeling that one had to be special, and I was even more determined that I should become someone of substance and emulate such great leaders. Even the morning newspapers would bring to the fore leaders who were spirited and had so much to offer. However, much as I tried, I could not relate to anyone, for they all seemed so far away. Till I met someone who was a leader I could relate to; one who was an everyday leader.

She was a simple and friendly person but not charismatic—far from it. She had some medical issues that had caused weight gain. She certainly did not seem to be someone from whom one could learn much. She was always smiling, and her good cheer brought smiles to others. I often wondered: what was the source of her happiness?

We met in my office and chatted a bit. She was paid a reasonable salary, but her expenses were always more than her earnings. She spent almost a third of it on her child, who was at a school nearby. I was always curious to know how she managed her money. Fortunately, she did not have to pay rent, since her one-room apartment was paid for; something for which she is grateful to her community.

Clearly, she had a purpose—to give her daughter the best possible education, make sure she did well at her school, and support her as a parent and give her a happy life. Something all of us do. What was different was her fervour and her vision. She was ever smiling and laughing despite her life's challenges. She put passion in all she did and was diligent and caring. She was very client-centric and juggled several things at once, even under severe pressure. Weekends found her still keeping a watch on things. Her silver bullet was her communication—keeping her clients informed and on top of things. Many staff members and managers would rush to her when they needed help. One day, I invited her to write something on my whiteboard, and she wrote an inspiring quote. I would wait each day for her to write a few lines on my whiteboard. She would always leave something on my whiteboard for me to ponder. She was a quintessential giver.

The pandemic hit her family very hard. Her husband lost his lifelong job with his firm, and suddenly he had to look out for himself. The strength of her spirit was evident in the ease with which she took it upon herself to not only support him but also give a sense of direction to him and the family. She suggested he start a small shop catering to the needs of the colony that they lived in. It was a hard time; things were looking difficult. Curfew meant that customers could not come to the shop. He had to go and deliver the goods. She was always looking for ways to make each rupee stretch a little bit farther. Her husband found himself in what he thought was a strange situation: he was being supported by his wife. His ego took a small beating, but it was all good.

Back to her. She had been suffering from her weight issues for a long time, but she had done nothing about it. Now, she decided to take up weight loss as a challenge. She got herself a Fitbit lookalike and started to walk. She walked like a person possessed, almost ten miles a day, every day. That meant waking up at four-thirty in the morning. She did it for ten months. She had found a good friend in one of the 'keep fit' guys, who taught her the power of self-restraint and discipline. She was feeling better and looked better too. She was happy with her progress. She took pictures of herself, the 'before and after' kind. Her social media handles got some major traction. She was one of the top three in the firm in the Weight Loss Challenge. She was proud of her achievement. She had lost twenty-two kilos. We were proud of her. Leading that pack was her reporting manager, someone who believed in her. He knew that she would come out on top.

Her determination is perhaps the secret behind her smiles. She is an inspiring leader. I can relate to such people. They are real, alive; people whom you can see and say to yourself: they are true leaders. She had a vision for herself, a vision for her family. She did not give up. She drew on her resources, relied on friends to help her find a way. Always positive. And all along, she kept smiling, knowing that someone would certainly smile upon her one day. She manages her life, her work, family and people around her. She has a quality that defines leaders—resilience.

My apologies; I forgot to introduce her. At work she is called an executive assistant—a secretary. I call her a leader at work, and beyond. I have so much to learn from her. Benny is an inspiring leader, she is.

3

Leadership on the Fly

I live in the city of Hyderabad. My workplace is in Mumbai. I keep shuttling between the cities, between work and home. This was before the pandemic. Travel is hard; not easy to master. You are at the mercy of the elements some months of the year. On some days, you are at the mercy of the airlines. Flights don't always depart or arrive on time. I was quite used to delayed flights and had an almost zen-like approach to such happenings. I would travel a day before so as to be ready for Monday, the start of the work week.

However, it was one of those crazy days. It was Sunday, and I usually catch a flight to Mumbai around six in the evening. It was always the same carrier so that I wouldn't get mixed up. I had to reach by 5 p.m. It was all set. For some reason, I booked an earlier flight, for 5.30 p.m., on Air India and forgot about it. As I headed to the airport, I got a call from the airline manager telling me that I was being offloaded as it was way past the boarding time of 4.30 p.m. I had completely forgotten that it was an earlier flight. Just by thirty minutes.

I reached the airport at 5 p.m. and rushed to the counter, where the reservation manager of Air India reiterated that I had been offloaded. My throat went dry. This had never happened to me, and I was feeling faint. I pleaded with the manager to see if he could manage something for me to catch the flight. He could see my anguish. He just stared at me, with a pitying look. It was clear to me that it was over, I could not catch the flight as the doors of the aircraft were shut. I was standing rooted to the spot, feeling foolish. I kept wringing my hands. I had no choice; I had to buy another ticket to Mumbai by another carrier.

I went to a couple of carriers and stood in long queues only to be told that all tickets to Mumbai were sold out. I would have to return home and try for a ticket for the following day. It was going to be embarrassing—I had to attend an important meeting in Mumbai in person. It was not a happy situation. It would also be impossible to secure a ticket the following day. It was the holiday season, and there was an unprecedented rush. It was at that moment that the manager who had taken me off the flight walked up to me and asked me if he could assist in getting me on another flight the same evening. I could have hugged him. It was very kind of him.

He got me to another carrier and said something to a staff member, and she readily had a ticket available for me for 6.30 pm that day. A miracle. She had refused me when I had met her earlier. I knew that the Air India manager, though not from that company, had exerted his influence to secure a ticket for me. It was an expensive ticket, and I gave my credit card to the attendant. Just when things started to look up, the attendant said that her card machine was not working and asked me for cash. She also told me that if I did not return with the cash on time, the sole ticket would be sold. Those were the days post demonetization, and ATMs were running dry. I ran from one ATM to another and finally, after three dry ATMs, I managed to get cash. I kissed the ATM! I ran back and gave the money to the woman at the counter only to be told that the last ticket was taken. My pleas fell on deaf ears, for she was clear: first come, first served. She did not make the slightest effort to help. Just my luck.

Back to my benefactor. The AI manager asked me to wait and said he would try again. He told me that it would be difficult. I thanked him and told him that I would wait for him. Ten long minutes passed and then I got a call from the manager, asking if I could meet him. He had managed to get me a ticket for the regular 6.30 p.m. flight, the one I had tried for earlier but was told it was running full. And he had got it at the normal price. He had not given up. He had been working silently all along to get me a ticket and that too at regular price. The same routine, rush to the manager—and he was waiting with the ticket in his hand. I did not even have to stand in a queue. I just handed him the money.

I thanked Sumit Trivedi. That was his name. I was amazed at this man. He helped someone he did not know. He saw someone in distress and did what he thought he should do—help. For over half an hour, he had relentlessly worked his charm on the staff at a different carrier in order to secure a ticket for me. I was at a loss of words. Why would someone do this for anyone? I asked him what I could do for him. I had taken his phone number to ensure that I connected with him. We heard the call for boarding for my flight, and there was still security to clear. I looked at Sumit Trivedi, seeking an answer to my question—what could I do for him? He simply said, 'Sir, please fly Air India each time, every time.' I hugged him warmly and walked away in awe of the man. He had mastered the art of service beyond self.

I wish I could be a Trivedi to someone, for by his focus and service orientation, Trivedi had demonstrated leadership beyond compare. And leadership starts with the spirit of service.

4
Of Sour Grapes, Conviction and Vision

Many years ago, Ram, a friend, surprised a lot of us by declaring that he was going into farming—to grow grapes. He was a successful engineer and was well-known for his keen eye and his penchant for being perfect. So, for Ram to turn to farming, it was an eye-popping move. His friends tried to cajole Ram against this move, but he said, 'What is life if I don't take a chance? I'll never be able to do this again. I'm young enough to take this risk'. I was not a big influence on Ram but was supportive of what he was doing. Ram put in all his life's savings and bought himself a parcel of land somewhere near Shamirpet on the outskirts of Hyderabad. Ram was a determined man. He spent a lot of time researching farming and its methods. He set up a small shack for the farmhands to stay in and did all that he needed to do to get a good crop. He would spend hours training them and explaining his scientific methodologies.

He plunged into growing grapes. He had done enough research about them. He knew what temperature, what soil and what amount of water they needed. He would have four varieties of grapes, he said to me proudly. Two of them were table varieties, and two were for the wineries. He was very confident. It was an expensive investment. To top it all, he had no control over the temperature, and a whole year's work could be destroyed in an instant if the rain gods were not kind to him. He said he had sheltered them in special canopies. He used to speak to them each day. He was practically cut off from all of us. He gave up his workshop to his partners, who ran it in his absence. He was at peace with his grapes. We never asked him about the grapes, as we were not sure if this was a good thing to speak about.

I met him a few years later and asked him, 'Ram, how are the grapes?' He proudly opened a small box of grapes. I popped one into my mouth and almost spat it out—it was sour. Was this all he had to show after eight years of toil, I thought. He smiled in a knowing way. 'I just manage to survive by selling a few boxes of these to my people who work at the farm.' He said that the winery took a few crates from him, but they were not good at paying him on time. I asked 'Where is your life going? Do you seriously want to pursue this?' He said he was convinced it was the right thing for him to do. He was not making money, but he was firm that he would continue farming. He said that he felt at peace with himself. He loved sleeping under the stars, he said. He was loyal to all his workmen at the farm. It was an affirmation of his faith in his farm. I asked him to stick to his convictions and not waver a bit. I felt a bit awkward even as I left Ram to his farm. Sometimes in our careers, we do something risky born out of our convictions. But was it the right thing to do? I was unsure but what could I tell Ram? The only thing I told him was that he needed to keep his eyes open to opportunities—in a vague kind of way. What I was certain about Ram was his convictions.

I recently met Ram and nothing much seemed to have changed with him or his farm. He seemed ebullient, as always. I asked him if he was doing well. Almost as if it was a certain question that he was ready for, he gave me a bunch of grapes to taste and asked me, 'What do you think of these grapes?' This time I was honest with him and said, 'These grapes are sour. How will this ever sell? How will it work for you?' 'Yes buddy, I know, but they seem to work for me,' he replied smilingly. It didn't make any sense to me. Ram was like that: enigmatic. You never knew what was on his mind. He was mild-mannered but deep. Remember, he was an engineer, and a good one at that. I could not understand his response and looked at him quizzically.

Ram explained, 'The grapes haven't done very well, but the land that grows these grapes seems to have done a lot better—something I had kept in mind.' He had bought two parcels of land alongside the highway. The price of land had shot up to astronomical levels. He had sold the smaller piece and bought himself a house and bought more land in another place. He still retained the bigger piece of land for growing grapes. He thanked me for giving him the courage to have faith in his own convictions and said that the land had turned into gold! He was smiling from ear to ear.

I left the farm feeling happy for Ram and was lost in thought about what courage and conviction can do for life and careers. There must have been so many trials and tribulations in his life, so many years of doubting Thomases and a long barrage of questions he had to get through. And I guess Ram just dug in and stuck it out. What is life without risk in it? Life is to be lived a bit on the edge, and in doing so, it is convictions that tease out the results. However unintended, positive consequences play out for the brave. He gave up the life of the city and lived his dream. He wanted to make money, but more, he wanted to make good grapes.

Ram still believes that one day he will produce grapes that aren't sour. I am convinced he will. His vision of his land has paid off, for sure. To me, Ram is a simple man with a simple vision for himself, and with a conviction beyond compare.

5

Of All the Things You Build, You Build People

She was a confident lady, if I have ever seen one, this Archana; articulate and professional. She had everything in her to be successful. I met her after she joined as a young manager on a team that was rapidly expanding. She was someone you could rely on to do the most difficult of tasks and someone who would not come back to you seeking every set of small instructions to get the task sorted out. She was independent, and many around her looked up to her as a woman of substance. She has her own set of followers—all young professionals who admired her spirit and her focus. Such was Archana.

Archana worked for a tough manager from my team, a no-nonsense kind of guy. He was a bit rough around the edges, result-oriented, and had no time for the niceties of the day. He also did not respond to the customary 'good mornings' or 'good afternoons'. He was always busy and always in a bit of a hurry. He would not listen to anyone. He was bent on getting things done and had a tough exterior. On and off, I used to tell him to relax and smell the roses—when he found the time, that is. He was a bit of a maverick, but his clients loved him. They loved his results. He was good at his stakeholder management. He had his failings, of course. For one, I was not sure if he made a good boss. Archana was not his favourite. She was all at sea with this guy. Both of them were cut from the same cloth, I guess. Months passed by, and it was time for the year-end performance reviews.

I opened my inbox early in the morning and was surprised to see Archana's resignation mail. This was a bolt from the blue! I had not expected it, and it had come without any heads up. I pushed aside everything else on my schedule and asked for her to see me. She sat in front of me and looked me in the eye and said that she was quitting—she had had 'enough of it'. I tried my charm on her, all of my persuasion, all my listening. She was adamant about quitting. She was rated as 'unsatisfactory', and that had hurt her to the quick. She was leaving as she felt unappreciated. It was the days of the downturn and the economy was not kind to those looking for another job. Knowing this, I gently asked if she had a job lined up, given that these were difficult times. The ego in her response startled me. She was as adamant as ever about leaving. I approached my neighbour, Divakar, a colleague and a wise man, and sought his help to talk her out of her resignation. I would feel sad to see such a person leave us.

Divakar was a good man. He said it was an uphill task to retrieve the situation. He initiated a conversation with her. It was a long one. Somewhere in the discussions, he asked if she wished to be successful and 'top-rate' again, and her eyes shone. I knew that the ice was broken. Divakar said that it would be great to prove to us that she was indeed of such mettle and that she should take up the challenge. She relented. Divakar then took it upon himself to build her confidence back. He spent hours with her over many months, listening to her, coaching her, mentoring her. A year passed, and it was time for the dreaded year-ends again. I tried to meet Divakar to check on Archana and her performance. He was unavailable. He and I excused ourselves from the process of evaluation as we would have undue influence over it. We left it to the team and her manager to evaluate on merits.

When the results were at my desk, I was not surprised. Archana stood tall as a top performer. It was a unanimous choice of the elders in the room who conducted the consensus meetings on the evaluation of performance. She had had an outstanding year. Her manager, who had been her baiter, was her cheerleader. The results would be released in a week, and there was tension in the air. A week later, she came to meet us. I could see that she was in tears—tears of joy. She sat in front of me, and I could see the resurgence of her spirits. She had found her edge, her confidence. And her life. I congratulated her and walked her to the door. Many in the workstations nearby stood up and applauded. They knew as well. I went over and hugged Divakar, her coach and mentor. Of the many things you build, the one of lasting value is building people.

6

Lighting a Lamp of Hope

When trouble comes calling, it descends in a tsunami. She was a sprightly girl once, working in a great firm with fine friends. She was someone everyone wanted to know and get close to. She was always respectful and had a point of view that was different from others. She presented these in a gentle way, and we admired her for the ease of her conversation on the most contentious of issues, all done so effortlessly. We even asked her how she managed it, and she would give a broad smile exuding charm, and we knew that she was not going to speak about it. We were happy to know her, but as she generally kept to herself, we did not know anything about her beyond her work. I knew she lived with her parents, who were on the wrong side of sixty. She was devoted to them and, as in most Indian households, they were worried about her and wanted her to 'settle down'.

One day, she came up to me to let me know that she had got married over the weekend. Just at that moment, she did not seem to be the person that I knew. She could have at least invited us to her wedding, I thought. She said that she got married to someone in Singapore and had to relocate. So, she had come by to let me know that she was leaving the firm. I asked her if she was happy that she was relocating. She was not sure, she said. She was worried about her parents, and that was on her mind. She did not mention why her office friends and colleagues were not invited to the wedding. In her quiet way, she left the firm and went her way. Time passed.

It was not a happy marriage. It was not working out in Singapore. They separated. She had never lived on her own and, in any case, not overseas. Not one to give up easily, she found a job in a good multinational company. Life moved on, and things seemed to be going well for her and she was feeling comfortable with the way life was unfolding for her. She still worried about her parents. Then the proverbial tsunami struck. One day, as she was walking toward the arrival station of the metro, she just slumped to the ground. Luckily, she was near the steps of the subway. A kind woman rushed her to the hospital, where she was diagnosed with cancer. As if that were not enough, she was running out of precious money. Her firm was not in a position to fund her hospital expenses on a perpetual basis. Life was bleak. Fast forward, she was moved to the Tata Cancer Hospital in Mumbai.

Her close friend Vinay, who had also been her reporting manager in the firm that she had quit, came to know of this. He called me up, and the two of us decided to visit her. Vinay had stuffed an envelope in his shirt pocket. He was not the hospital-going chap and was scared of such places. He had been to hospitals before; their strong smell of antiseptic evoked fear in him. He had been hospitalized for a few weeks when he was in kindergarten, and that experience had traumatized him. I was far stronger. We reached the place and met the girl's parents. We were all emotional and teary-eyed. Vinay found it difficult to cope with all the tugging to his heartstrings. Her parents pointed us to a hospital ward in the distance. It was a long walk to the ward.

The ward of a cancer hospital is not easy to walk through. There were beds on either side, and young and old were propped up on pillows of pain. There were stifled moans and groans. It was difficult to look either side of the passage, at these beds of anguish. We still had to look for her. Finally, we found her. There she was, in the last bed, the one near the wall. She lay on the bed, almost reduced to a skeleton. It was difficult to speak to her, and she tried her best to avoid any eye contact. She was silent. She was emaciated and could hardly whisper. Her parents had spoken of an incessant back pain.

Vinay and I had decided we would do something for her. 'We need her to hang on to something,' Vinay had said when we first spoke about it. Now, he looked at her and reached into his coat pocket and pulled out an envelope. He waved the envelope and said to her, 'This is an appointment letter waiting for you, dear Mohana, and we don't have all the time in the world. Your team is missing you. So, get well soon and I will see you at work in a month. I hope you got that.' He did not wait for her response. Just turned around and walked out. Scared, I guess. I noticed tears welling up in her eyes. I stayed back a few minutes, held her hand. No words were spoken. And yet a poignant conversation ensued. And yes, tear drops from her eye. We left. She had managed a weak smile. Much later, she told her parents that post our visit, her racking pain seemed more tolerable.

Mohana did return to work in her old firm. It took her a few months to recover from the dreaded illness. Her ebullience was back, and so was her quiet cheer. She continued to dazzle people with her professionalism and humanness. All it took was a couple of gentlemen to infuse a sense of purpose and let her know that she was valued, that she was needed. They went there to light the lamp of hope, to feed the faith that holds life, in a caring way. It worked. Faith heals, and hope feeds that faith. One needs purpose to live; a life of purpose. And it takes a leader to infuse a sense of purpose. Be it even life.

Did I mention that Mohana is now a CHRO of a leading company?

7
Diversity at Work

I had read a book in my college days, called *What on Earth Evolved? ... In Brief* by Christopher Lloyd. It spoke about the top 100 species that changed the world. I can wager that you will find it difficult to guess the top three! They are the earthworm, algae and cyanobacteria, followed by rhizobia, lactobacillus and, in sixth place, humans. This left a deep impression on me. I could never have guessed that the earthworm is the most important of species that changed the world. To extrapolate, how can I learn from leaders around me, ordinary people who are making a deep impression all around themselves?

Murali was a competitor in my MBA days in XLRI, Jamshedpur, a top B-school. He was always top of the class, and my only goal was to better my grade point index to get past him. He seemed so much in control in all that he did. He was wise, calm and composed. We were good friends and had a healthy respect for each other. Once, it so happened that in a nearby university there was a debate competition, and Murali had signed up for it. I had not registered on time and could not participate. The leader, Murali, in this case, had a choice of picking one more person from our class, as it was a two-member team. Murali was looking around and had passed on the word that he was hunting for the second member of his team. I was sure that Murali would pick me. We would make a formidable team, I reckoned. After all, we were top of the class and were strong in our own ways.

I came to the cafeteria and there was a lot of buzz all around. A lot of my classmates were looking at me and speaking in hushed tones with each other. I was curious and went up to the nearest table to check what was going on. I then learnt that Murali had picked John Christian. I was very upset that I was not chosen; hugely disappointed. My conceited self kept telling me that I was better than John. My ego would not accept that John was as good as I was. Murali and John went to the nearby town and came back with a huge cup. They were the winners. All of us went up to Murali and John and congratulated them. Of course, my ego came in the way of a heartfelt acknowledgement of their success. I was puzzled. How could Murali ignore me? I swallowed my pride and went up to him and asked him to explain himself and his success. He said simply: 'I wanted a diverse team. You and I are more of the same. John brought in a different aspect of creativity, something that we both lack. Diverse thinking won, I guess.' Murali was so right. I congratulated him and walked on in amazement of his sagacity at such a young age. I never forgot that moment; it is precious.

Getting Better

The two most important days in your life are the day you were born and the day you find out why.

—Mark Twain

Many things happen in any single day. Some of them leave a lasting memory. They shine a light on what happens, albeit in a limited way, which leads to life-altering ways of working and living. A simple word or two, perhaps from a mentor. Part of mentoring is about sponsoring—standing up for your people. These are stories about leaders who show the way, and how we learn from very 'ordinary' people—a secretary or the driver who cleans the car. There are inspiring ways to read about the selfless many who work, for they believe in service before self.

We also learn by just listening. By observing. Things that happen around us. Small things that influence the way we think and act. Small acts that make a big impact on us. Cues that make a big difference to others' lives. Influence is perhaps about allowing us the liberty of being influenced or influencing others, all in a positive way. Getting better is about making progress each day. Inching along. Slowly, but surely.

1
A Bittersweet Pill

A long time ago, I used to work in a small town. It was a mining area, and I worked at a factory that made explosives for the mining industry. We lived in a colony that was a short distance from the office and the factory. Work ended at around five in the evening. We all left the factory at almost the same time. The town had a few shops around my office: a few shops dispensing grocery, and a few dispensing medicines. It was a small town. What was wonderful about it was that we knew each other, and it was always nice how we addressed each other in a familiar way. Such is the charm of a small town.

As a normal practice, while I was leaving work for home, I used to call my wife to ask if there was anything, such as groceries, to be purchased on the way home. It wasn't easy going to the bazaar after a long day's work. Once I got home, I would have my cup of tea and then put up my feet in the balcony and enjoy the view of a small lake in front of my company-provided house. Nothing could take me away from those few moments of bliss with the calm waters and birds chirping before the evening light died out.

My mother had come to stay with us, and she was unwell. I had asked the doctor and he had advised some medicines. I was given the prescription in the morning and knew that I had to purchase the medicines. This was easy, I told myself. It was a common medicine, and there were four medical stores on the way home. I don't know if I am the only one who can get distracted when I am on the road and driving. I was thinking of the tea at home and unsure about what my wife would have as accompaniment for the tea. Would it be biscuits, or would it be something special? I was daydreaming. I was on my scooter, and as I passed the first one, I realized I had missed stopping to check for the medicines.

I told myself that there were three more pharmacies along the way, and it would not be hard to find the medicine at the next pharmacy. I was lost in thought and angry with myself, and even before I realized it, I missed the second one as well. The third pharmacy was overcrowded. I was impatient to get home and decided to go to the fourth, the one closer to home but a long way from the overcrowded third pharmacy.

I stopped at the fourth shop. As I walked in and uttered the medicine's name, with a prescription that I carried with me and waved at the chemist, the salesperson cheerfully said that it was not available and advised me to go to the 'other shop'. Wondering what there was to be so cheerful about in the unavailability of a medicine, I moved to the other shop, the third, the one that was quite crowded. I had to wait for some time and finally got to the counter, where a pharmacist looked at my prescription and smiled at me. He said it was not available. He added that it would be available in a couple of days. He suggested that I go to another shop that was some distance away. Reluctantly, I got on my scooter and went to the second shop. The same set of actions. The wait to get to the counter, the prescription, and finally being told that it was not available. And, of course, the helpful suggestion to go to the 'other shop'. It was the first shop, the one that was just outside my office. I was feeling foolish. I had to retrace my steps all the way to the office. I was utterly upset and annoyed. I was praying now and hoping that they stocked the medicines.

I went up to the counter and to the chemist and gave him the prescription. I was looking at him anxiously, for I feared I would be running out of luck if even he did not have the medicines. He took one look at the prescription and asked some quick questions to check if this was for a senior citizen. He smiled, walked to a counter and pulled out a box, rummaged through it and fished out the right medicines. I was told that the medicines were rare but he luckily had them. At last, I got my medicines at this shop, went outside and hopped on to my scooter and headed home.

As soon as I reached home, I gave my wife the medicines. She asked me what had taken me so long. I was getting irritated with her; however, I kept my cool. I just asked my wife to pour me a cup of tea. She asked me if all was well. I smiled and told her that I had to figure out something for myself. As I sipped the tea in silence, I was thinking what message had life in store for me. What was the lesson of the day? What was it that I was learning from this experience? One can get philosophical over tea, I guess.

Perhaps it was about taking the first opportunity that life presents and not to wait or procrastinate. Things are simple at first, when 'done and dusted' quickly. Keep life simple—do things now! Sometimes it is the smallest of things that bring the biggest misery, something that could cause you great pain. What first seemed simple could become complicated and cause anxieties. It was a bittersweet pill that I will never forget in my life. I always buy at the first medicine shop on the way home. And that goes for many things, and it is a continuous learning. Would this apply to buying groceries? I need to find out.

2

Of Advice: Received—and How!

I am just amazed at the amount of free advice that is given out and received each day—all well-intended, and some very profound. Some is said in jest but is precious all the same. So, I decided to count how many pieces of advice I received a day, or heard about.

'Get up early; it makes you healthy, wealthy and wise,' said my sleepy wife. It was six in the morning. The fact that she was still lazing in bed is something that I will avoid speaking about. That morning, I met my friend, Ganesh, from Mumbai, and he mentioned quite casually that the best advice he received was from his colleague, Kumar, who asked him to sell his bike if he were to go to Mumbai. This seemed to be everyday advice anyone would give, but not for Ganesh. This called for his giving up something he really loved—his bike. And yet, he knew that there was some truth in the advice because, given his health condition, he could not afford to take chances. He said that over the years, he could count off many near-misses he has had on the roads—even in the car or the cab he was sitting in, and how he always remembered Kumar for it. Advice, oftentimes, is not what you want to hear!

That afternoon at the office, I met my colleague of many years, Ravi, and he said he received the best advice from his boss. He had asked him to 'add some focus and commitment to life' and, as an example, asked him to work on buying a house. Ravi had told him that he did not have the kind of money that was needed to purchase a house—it was beyond his means. His boss made a comment in jest that most things were 'within your grasp, beyond your reach', and that he should try regardless. Today, Ravi is the proud owner of a flat in Mumbai, and the appreciation over the years (pun intended) knew no bounds. He was ever grateful to his manager.

This was beginning to get interesting. I had not solicited any stories of advice, and yet they were coming my way! That same afternoon, Venkat, a head-hunter, called me. I remember him well, as I remember I had received the best advice from him several years ago. He had told me: 'You don't get ahead of the pack by being a rolling stone, so don't change your jobs every two to three years.' It was invaluable advice. How can I ever thank him enough? Incidentally, Venkat called me to let me know that he had changed his job. Ironic.

I came home a little early that evening. The maid was engrossed in her cleaning. She was a stickler for cleanliness. She was almost burnishing the banister that led to the landing on the first floor. It was made of wood, and I was intrigued by her diligence. I lauded her for it. She responded that it was her duty to 'do simple things exceedingly well'. I used to think I was good, but Chandra was the guru. Here she was, giving me some sage advice in a graceful way. I was touched.

Later that evening, I met my children. I was hunched over my computer, trying to belt out a proposal, and was lost in thought. Vignesh patted me on my shoulder and said 'You got to relax, Dad!' and walked away. Vivek, the elder, came in a few minutes later and added, 'Dad, you've got to chill!' That was a lot of advice in one day already. I called my mother, who lived in Chennai; one of my regular calls, as I was living in another city, Hyderabad. Post the pleasantries, she asked me to take care of my health. Big hugs, Mom! Advice was raining on me. My wife, Chitra, asked me about the call, and I was lost in thoughts about my mother. Chitra asked me not to 'think too much' but remain 'in the moment'. This was a family pack of advice—precious indeed! I was overwhelmed. It appeared that in a day, one gets a lot of advice. Some intended and some unintended.

In sum and substance, here was the world reaching out to me. The world cares, people care, friends care, family cares, and just about anyone you meet—they all care for you. They all express it in different ways. We like some of the advice we get, some we don't. I recognize that if anyone gives any advice, it is because they care! I felt good.

A dear friend called me and advised me to pen my thoughts. Even as I write this, I am beaming with the joy of gratitude for a day well spent—heeding the priceless advice ... of the priceless!

3

This Was for That and That Was for This!

Very early in my career, I had a boss who was an incredibly nice man. I was working as an industrial relations officer in a factory that manufactured explosives for use in the coal mines. This was in the heart of what was then Bihar. The trade unions were everywhere, and the union leaders ruled the roost. The factory had recently seen some violent activity by the union leaders, and there was some tension in the air. There used to be union elections on a periodic basis, and the factory would break into a flurry of activity around elections. We used to ask the workers to keep the elections outside the office and factory premises, and although there were tall promises, there would always be a rub-on effect on the behaviour of those who were candidates, and of course, when a new member was elected, I could notice the change in many around me. Post elections, we had a new union leader. Let us call him Ishwar.

Pathak was our cashier. Each month, the cashier would count the salary amounts and hand over a pay packet to each of the workmen. It was a laborious task. It needed care and caution, for there could be no mistake. There were neither note-counting machines in those days, nor ATMs that fed out cash when called upon. Pathak, the cashier who had worked with the company for over thirty years, handed over a pay packet to the new union leader, Ishwar. Even as he started counting the notes, he suddenly claimed that 100 rupees were missing. The average salary in those days was about Rs 1300. So, 100 rupees missing meant a big loss for Ishwar, and he made a big hullaballoo, directing profanity at Pathak, and asked all the employees to stop taking their salaries. A big scene ensued. Pathak kept pleading that he was not at fault and said that he was a very careful man. A slanging match ensued, and Ishwar started shouting at the top of his voice and blaming it on the 'management', saying that it was all planned to 'show the union its place'. Ishwar had started well, indeed.

The matter reached the ears of my general manager, Om Prakash, also known as O.P. He was a kind man. He was very sharp, and behind his kind eyes was a brilliant mind. He knew Pathak to be an honest man, but he wanted to defuse the situation. So, O.P. called Ishwar to his office so as to not make a scene at the finance enclosure. Ishwar insisted that he was paid 100 rupees less. O.P. then called Pathak separately and quizzed him. Pathak said that he was innocent and that he had served as a cashier for over thirty years. O.P. told Pathak to compensate the same amount from his account. Pathak was in tears, as this had never happened in his long career and it was a blotch on his impeccable record. Everybody forgot about the incident except Pathak. He was confident that it was the mischief of the union leader. We all knew that Pathak was right, but the damage was done. Pathak was seen as a mischief-maker, a union-baiter. Life was difficult for him in the colony where his co-workers lived. He could not go to the cafeteria either.

The following month, prior to pay day, my boss, O.P., called Pathak and said something to him. I knew that he would advise Pathak to be careful. The cashier's area was abuzz that Ishwar was coming for his pay-packet. Everyone was waiting at strategic points to see what would happen. It almost seemed that history was repeating itself. This time again, the same 100 rupees was missing, and Ishwar created an even bigger ruckus—it was the same old ritual. People were very upset that this was happening to Ishwar. For his part, Ishwar gave his pay packet to others to take a look. By then, O.P. had been told about the trouble, and he came out of his office.

O.P. went to the cashier's area. As soon as he reached the place, he noticed that there were a lot of employees milling around the place. He looked at Ishwar and said, 'Why is it only your cover has 100 rupees less, every month? This never happens to anyone else but you. Pathak has been here for ages! Will you doubt your fellow being each time? Besides, don't forget that he is also part of your union. Why would he do this to his leader?' Ishwar was muttering something, but his voice was lost in the collective noise about the place.

O.P. then looked at the crowd of people and, in a measured voice, said to them that Pathak was a fine cashier and that he had never ever been at fault in his illustrious career. So saying, he left the place. The crowd did some internal consultation and they all looked at Pathak, and they then shouted at Ishwar, accusing him of being an unfit union leader who found fault with his own staff members. Ishwar had no answer and went away, his pay packet 100 rupees lighter.

That evening, I was with O.P. in his office, going over some factory personnel matters. There was a knock, and Pathak entered. He grasped O.P.'s hands and thanked him profusely. Seeing the bewilderment on my face, O.P. said he trusted Pathak. He then thanked Pathak for his work, and I could see in Pathak a very thankful man. He then left and kept on thanking O.P. Pathak looked at me and said that I should learn from O.P. about justice and being fair. I did not understand and, of course, by then the cashier, Pathak, had left the room. I looked at O.P. questioningly. O.P. said that he knew that Ishwar was out to create trouble when he claimed the first time that he had got less money. Pathak had a stellar record of perfect dispensing of cash. He trusted Pathak. All O.P. told him earlier was that the next time he prepared the pay envelopes, Pathak was to put 100 rupees less in Ishwar's pay packet. The trick was to appeal to the people about Pathak's innocence. Given the reputation of the cashier, the people would be sure that Pathak was innocent. And it worked. Ah, what drama! That day, Pathak went home walking tall, his reputation restored. I went back home feeling lighter and with a new respect for my boss, O.P.

Sometimes it pays to pay someone back in their own coin. After all, 'This was for that and that was for this!'

4
Some Terrible Times, Some Wonderful Actions

It was one of those difficult days, Ram knew, as he slowly made his way to his workstation. People were hesitant to come to him. It was one of those days of decision, where he had to decide if the work done by one of the team members was good enough for him to carry on in the organization. Not an easy task.

Ram was ambivalent. In good times, things are good. When times are bad, everything looks terrible. He knew he was being watched. He read through the files slowly. It was clear that the team member was an underperformer. Sometimes, you need the support of those around you, and the person had none. He had to let the person know that he was not good enough for the role and perhaps even needed to separate from the firm.

It was a difficult choice. He went up and told his manager and sought his counsel. The manager was only too happy to let the person separate. Ram was not convinced, though. He called the team member to his office and heard him out. He first pointed out what the person was good at and what he was failing to do. He told him that he would give him one last chance. More, he would help him along the path of the 'performance improvement plan'. There was a weary smile of gratitude. Ram, of course, was worried.

Ram went to the coffee shop nearby. It was a long day. Although he had his manager's approval to terminate the services of a person, he had not. He felt burdened with the thought—have I done right? Would his manager forgive him, as he had not told him about his decision? He was lost in thought.

Just then, a hand fell on Ram's shoulder. His manager's. He was smiling. 'So, you gave him a lease of life, did you?' he asked. He did not wait for an answer. He simply said, 'Ram, you are a good man. It is the right answer. Not easy, but the right answer.' So saying, he smiled again in a warm sort of way and left.

What stayed with Ram were the manager's words—words that brought life into Ram's world. Words have a power to elevate. These would not be forgotten in a long time. He smiled and coifed his cup. He thought of the words of encouragement he would remember a long time; words that would enliven someone's life as much as his own had been: 'You are a good man.' In our lows, we cling to words. Words that enliven our lives. Words that get us to be better.

5

Of Faith and Target Practice

I was part of a team that represented my college in rifle shooting as part of the National Cadet Corps (NCC). We had to travel almost thirty kilometres to a firing range every morning, and this extended even to the weekends. Our coach, Major Sairangan, was a remarkable guy—a man of great character and principle.

One Saturday, Major Sairangan called us to the shooting range very early in the morning, and we were up there at 6 a.m. in our uniform, but the rifles hadn't arrived and the ammunition was to be brought by Major Sairangan. The firing ranges of our days were quite different from the ones that you see today. It was a huge open field, and there was a hill on the horizon. There were no trees around, and the place was completely barren. It was fenced off to ensure that there was no casualties.

We were waiting out in the sun for Major Sairangan. Six became nine, which became twelve, which became three in the afternoon, and there was no trace of the major. We didn't want to leave the place, because we knew if he said he would come, he *would* come! In those days, we didn't have mobile phones, but the spoken word was more powerful than anything else. There was a certain connect with Major Sairangan. We had huge faith in the major, as we knew him to be a man of his word. It was well past lunchtime, but still nobody wanted to move out of the place. It was almost four—we were hungry, irritated and terribly tired.

At five o'clock, a rickety army van arrived at the range. Major Sairangan bounced out of the vehicle. He was dishevelled and his clothes were dirty. The first thing he said was, 'Folks, let's unload the materials and start shooting.' We started unloading and getting ready for target practice. There was no mention of the reason of his being late or thanking us for waiting for him. By the time we set up the targets and started shooting, it was half past five in the evening and getting dark. We could hardly see, but all our coach said was if we were to fire by the candle light, we would. And we fired away. Would you believe it—we had the best group score ever! Although we could hardly see the target, we scored our best. At last, when we could see almost nothing, we stopped firing and packed up.

Finally, when everything was done, the major opened up: 'Boys, I am very proud of you! You had the faith in me. You waited and you knew that I would come. I just want to tell you that my truck broke down in a remote area, and it was a desolate place. So, I had to repair the vehicle myself. I went down to the town to get the parts, came back and fixed the broken axle myself. That's why I was late. By the way, I have brought some food for you. I knew you would all wait for me. Thank you.'

That evening, as I sat down, I realized how extremely important it is to have faith in yourself and trust in your people. How you perform depends a lot on the kind of relationship you have with your teammates and your leaders. Relationships have a great way of testing you out. But if you have the resilience and the faith, then even on the darkest of days, when the sun is failing you, and your spirit is weak, faith in the relationship can get you the highest score and on target.

It is clear that we succeeded because we had the faith. There was a huge urge to let Major Sairangan know that we wanted to give our best. We didn't want to make him feel bad that it was because of him that we didn't fire well. We really wanted to show him that just as we had faith in him, he should have faith in us—that we would always give our best!

This is one story that will always remain with me as hugely inspiring. On any of my bad days, I recount this story and feel the palpable power of faith and trust, resilience and self-belief.

6

Playing to One's Strengths

My father was a good athlete in his days. He had a pair of running spikes—shoes that he got as a gift from Emil Zatopek, one of the greatest middle- and long-distance runners of his time. A triple crown holder, winner of the 5000 metres, 10000 metres and marathon at the 1952 Olympics. He had come to India, and my dad had the great privilege to meet him on the grounds of Loyola College, a famous institution of Chennai. Dad used to speak nineteen to the dozen about this meeting and how Emil told him about 'fartlek' training, which is a high-intensity interval training. I used to sit in fascination, listening to my father speaking about his meeting and how Emil was a down-to-earth man, how his English was not all that great but he was a giant of a man on the track. That was not all; when Emil left the college grounds, he asked for my father and gave him a pair of running shoes that had spikes in them. It was the single biggest possession for my father.

Fast forward. I wanted to be an athlete like my father. I went to my mother and told her that I was headed to the grounds and that I would return as an athlete one day. My mother was ever encouraging, and she told me to wear the spikes. Yes, the same spikes that had belonged to the great Emil. But they were too large for me. I told her that I could never fill the shoes of the great man and laughed. I reached the grounds and saw the coach. A self-appointed coach, he was unpaid, but it did not bother him. I wanted to be a sprinter. I went up to the coach and, with a tone of confidence in my voice, asked him if I could be a sprinter. He smiled and asked me to get 'on your mark' in the running lane. He had a timer and a clapper for a pistol. I was all ready to show him what a great sprinter I was. After all, my dad was a great athlete! I heard the sound go off and I ran, hell bent for leather. I breasted the tape at the end of the 100 metres. Huffing and puffing, I came back to the coach, and he showed me the stopwatch—it was all of fifteen seconds. He shook his head and told me that I could never make a good sprinter. I was crestfallen. I had practised a long time before I went up to be tested by the coach. I had tears in my eyes.

I came home and was sulking when my mother met me and asked me what the matter was. I told her that when I asked the coach if I could be a sprinter, he tested me and told me that I could never be one. She looked into my eyes and said deliberately, 'Wrong question, son. You should have asked him what you could be good at as a runner. Go back to him and ask him about it.' And be reverential about it, she added.

The following day, I went to the playground. The running lanes were demarcated with white powdered lime. I went up to the coach and touched his feet, and humbly asked him if he could help me and let me know what I could be good at. The old coach just smiled. He simply said to me, 'Keep running on the 400-metre track till I use this whistle.' I did not need any direction. I remember my father telling me that measured posture and consistent strides could help. I started running and must have run some fifteen rounds or so when I heard the whistle. After the first few rounds of the ground, I had lost count. I was enjoying the run. The shrill whistle brought me to a trot, and I ran towards the coach.

He smiled at me. He seemed impressed. He said that I could be a good long-distance runner if I put my mind to it. I needed some polishing on the turns and needed to get my strides a lot more even. I could not understand the rest of what he said. All I could figure out was that he saw a runner in me. I was happy. I touched his feet and packed up for the day. I reached home and ran straight to my mother. I told her about what the coach saw in me and then in a moment of joy, I just hugged her and said, 'Ma, you are the best coach! You asked me to ask the right question. Asking the right question was the turning point in my running.' I started to practise every day for at least two hours and sometimes twice a day. I was determined to bring the coach and my family something that they would remember, for they had invested in me. My coach was a hard man to please.

One day, I took the shoes that were presented to my father and showed them to him. I told him about their history. He had heard of Emil. He looked at it longingly. I also showed him two medals for the mile and the 5,000 metres at my college athletic events. He looked at me and gave me a hug and said that he knew that I had it in me to do well in long-distance running. I told him that my parents wanted him to have the shoes, as he had taught me something that was invaluable, and handed over the shoes to him. A pair of faded white shoes with shoelaces that had seen better days. It was a piece of history. He took them from me and gave me another hug and wished me well. A part of him was with me, and a part of me was now with him.

Long after, when I remembered this story, it had two important lessons for me—asking the right question and playing to strengths. I was unhappy that I was not a sprinter, till someone found a long-distance runner in me. Then having someone who insisted that I ask the right question. Perhaps in all ecosystems, there are a whole lot of people, with each one of them having a particular strength. All it takes is someone's faith and care that asks, tries and encourages strengths in people. Is this a tall ask, I ask myself.

7
Mother's Pickles

I always loved mother's pickles; the lemon ones were just finger-licking good. She took a lot of time preparing these. She would buy the lemons from the market, pressing each one gently to check the thickness of the rind. And her eyes would carefully bore into them, as if checking the juice content. Then she would cut them with her special knife and then rub salt into them and set them out to dry in the sun in special flat vessels, gently placing a fine cloth over them so the sun did not beat them up too much. Also, to keep away the birds. The next step would be mixing them with red chilli powder. Next, tossed in a very special mixture of condiments that were known only to her. She would never reveal them and said that I would not understand. I did not argue with her. I was more interested in laying my hands on them.

It was time for me to leave for Mumbai, and it was always a charade that played itself out with a lot of drama. I had my mother stay with us in Hyderabad, and that too with a lot of difficulty. She was a very independent woman. On Sunday afternoons, I would pack and leave to catch a flight to Mumbai in the evening. I had to tell her that I would be away for a week. It was easier telling my wife that I would be away for work. She understood; not my mother. She would argue that if I was going to travel this much, she should not have come to Hyderabad. My escape from such situations was to ask my son to go to her. One hug, and she would melt and sanity would prevail. I went to take her blessings before the trip, a ritual that I miss very much, for she is no more now. It was my way to let her know that I needed her, and she should stay with me. She suddenly said, 'Hey, I have something for you. She ran into the kitchen and put a small bottle of pickles on the table. Pickles were not something that you handed to someone. Sweets were allowed to be handed over, but pickles were not. She was that traditional. She asked me to take it with me. I loved that in her—the small, thoughtful things. Giving me things that I loved. I pushed it into my cabin luggage, grabbed my laptop bag and rushed to the cab waiting to take me to the airport. I reached the airport in time. The airlines had introduced severe checking at the airports, something new in those days. I was not aware of what I could carry and what I could not. In all ignorance, I forgot what I had placed in my bag, it went through the scanner and the security guard at the other end stopped me and asked me what I had in the bag. I had not anticipated this.

'My mother's homemade pickle,' I said with a sense of love and affection. He looked at me and said in a rather rude way that I could not take it in my handbag. I asked him how a pickle bottle could possibly hurt, and he was adamant. This is not going, he said. I tried all my ways of persuasion. He did not budge. 'Put this into the checked-in bag,' he said. I had nothing to check in, I pleaded. He was firm, as he should be. The queue was getting backed up owing to my argument over a 'silly pickle bottle', as he referred to it.

Then I started pleading with him and asked him if I looked like a person who could do any harm. My words fell on deaf ears, and he was getting irritated. Finally, in a rather sentimental way, I gifted the bottle to him, asking him to take it home and use it. I begged him not to throw it into the waste bin. It was my mother's gift to him, I said, and quickly added that he would thank mother if he tasted it. He gave me a blank stare and did not accept the gift of the pickle bottle. Just then, a smart young man in a white shirt asked me where I was going. I said I was flying to Mumbai. The man walked to the guard, said a few words and took the carefully packed bottle.

It was the commander of the flight I was taking to Mumbai. He said that he would take it with him for safekeeping in the pilot's cabin and would give it to me on landing. I could have hugged him. He nodded, as if understanding my feelings. The captain broke a rule for me, something I would never forget. Stepping up to break a rule to help another is part of setting a culture. Perhaps, in all that we do, we are all bound by rules that keep us straight. In a way, it defines the culture of the place—a disciplined one. It also made sure that the culture was preserved. All good; but there are times I have seen where in the breach of it all, a new culture emerges, one that is endearing.

Upon landing, I was called out and asked to come to the front of the aisle in the aircraft. There, the captain gave me the pickle bottle. He had gone out of his way to do something extraordinary for me. I was touched. I looked into his kind eyes and thanked him profusely. I asked him why he stepped out to do this for me. His eyes moistened, and he said that he had lost his mother a week ago. 'I know the value of love packed in a bottle of pickles,' he said. Instinctively, I hugged him. Then I took the bottle and walked away, my eyes welling up with tears.

Acknowledgements

This book has been written owing entirely to a number of people.

My friend, Subhomoy Das, a brilliant man who persuaded me to write and nudged me on.

My friends on social media, who constantly asked me to write a book. Their words of encouragement made me sit down to pen my thoughts. I hope they have bought the book.

Kanishka Gupta, a wonderful friend, who has an eye for all good things in life, and is elegant in all that he does.

My publisher, HarperCollins India, in particular, my editor Sachin Sharma, who guided me along the way. I could have never done this without him.

The brilliant teachers in my life, Fr McGrath of XLRI, Dr Indira Parikh, Late Dr Pulin Garg, Raghu Ananthanarayanan, Dr T.V. Rao. My wonderful bosses—O.P. Khetan, Ravindran G., Capt. Arvind Nautiyal, Daljit Singh, Ramesh Ramanathan, Pradeep Kar, Sanjay

Mashruwala, Dr Chandrasekhar Sripada, Tracey Edwards, Bob Chapman, P.R. Ramesh, Hari Kumar, V. Srikumar and N. Venkatram.

A special thanks to a few good friends—Naren, Sushanta Banerjee, Ashok Malhotra, Dr Arvind Agarwal, Satish Pradhan, Vikas Gupta, Ramesh Nandyala, Arun Rao, Madhu Vedula, Ekta, Benaifur Irani and Badari Narayana. Dr N.S. Rajan, S. Varajaranan, Vasu, Bharati, Surabhi—a big thanks. You have influenced me greatly.

My portals of learning—Vivekananda College, XLRI, and organizations: ICI, Sterling Holidays, Microland, Philips, Reliance and Deloitte. I have learnt so much from each one of you.

My wife, Chitra, my sheet anchor. She does not say much but is my staunchest critic and that helps me keep my feet firmly on the ground. My children, Vivek and Vignesh, Revathi, Bharati—all charming to a fault: I learn so much from them. Living life is what they teach me. My brother, Ganesh, my soulmate—thank you, da.

And all of you readers. You make a big difference to my life. Each of your purchases has gone to charity. You can write to me at nathansv@gmail.com, as I value your inputs.

About the Author

SV Nathan, a respected voice on human resources, is a partner and Chief Talent Officer of Deloitte India and serves on the Talent Executive Leadership of Deloitte Asia Pacific.

He is recognized as a 'Distinguished Alumnus' by XLRI, his alma mater, acknowledged as one of the Top Voices of LinkedIn and well known for his posts #OfficeTruths. He is a top HR influencer on social media.

He serves as the President of the National Human Resources Development Network (NHRDN), the largest body of HR professionals in India. He served in the past as Chair of Sumedhas, a not-for-profit education and research body devoted to learning through experience.

30 Years *of*

HarperCollins *Publishers* India

At HarperCollins, we believe in telling the best stories and finding the widest possible readership for our books in every format possible. We started publishing 30 years ago; a great deal has changed since then, but what has remained constant is the passion with which our authors write their books, the love with which readers receive them, and the sheer joy and excitement that we as publishers feel in being a part of the publishing process.

Over the years, we've had the pleasure of publishing some of the finest writing from the subcontinent and around the world, and some of the biggest bestsellers in India's publishing history. Our books and authors have won a phenomenal range of awards, and we ourselves have been named Publisher of the Year the greatest number of times. But nothing has meant more to us than the fact that millions of people have read the books we published, and somewhere, a book of ours might have made a difference.

As we step into our fourth decade, we go back to that one word – a word which has been a driving force for us all these years.

Read.

Harper Collins | 4th | HARPER PERENNIAL | HARPER BUSINESS | HARPER BLACK | हार्पर हिन्दी

HarperCollins *Children's Books* | HARPER DESIGN | HARPER VANTAGE | Harper Sport